C0-AJZ-261

750/510

PORTRAIT OF A PARISH PRIEST

By the same Author

★

BARBE ACARIE : WIFE AND MYSTIC
DON BOSCO

PRINT SOLD AT ARS DURING ABBÉ VIANNEY'S LIFETIME

PORTRAIT OF A PARISH PRIEST

St. John Vianney, the Curé d'Ars

by

LANCELOT C. SHEPPARD

THE NEWMAN PRESS

WESTMINSTER, MARYLAND

92
V65s

135515

NIHIL OBSTAT: ANDREAS MOORE, L.C.L.
CENSOR DEPVTATVS
IMPRIMATVR: E. MORROGH BERNARD
VICARIVS GENERALIS
WESTMONASTERII: DIE XXVI MARTII MCMLVIII

© Lancelot C. Sheppard 1958

PRINTED IN GREAT BRITAIN

CONTENTS

ILLUSTRATIONS

INTRODUCTION

WHEN he died in 1859 Jean-Marie-Baptiste Vianney was already popularly known throughout the world as the "Curé d'Ars". Since that date his fame has increased as the many biographies published in the course of the century have made him known to succeeding generations; his beatification in 1905, his canonization in 1925, have set the official seal of the Church on the popular veneration in which he has been held for more than a century. But it is still as the Curé d'Ars that he is known, rather than as St John Vianney, his description in the general calendar of the Roman rite on 9 August. He is venerated as a parish priest who found his way to heaven by employing the duties of his difficult position as the means to holiness.

It may be wondered why after the many biographies that have already appeared I should have thought it necessary to produce yet another. I have done so for several reasons. In the first place, in 1959 occurs the centenary of his death, and it is a fitting moment to consider him afresh in the light of the developments of a hundred years in human thought and the evolution of ideas. We are coming to see more clearly nowadays that the various marvellous (and, it should sometimes be added, odd) phenomena in the lives of the saints are not their most important claim to our attention. I have tried to deal with the many occurrences of this nature in the life of the Curé d'Ars, particularly the *Grappin*, in a way that, without doing violence to the facts, contains, it is hoped, the basis on which a possible explanation may be built up. The importance of a man like St John Vianney remains, however, in what he was and not in the marvels and somewhat puzzling phenomena connected with his life; principally, he is a sign for his times. In a very general sense, of course, saints are signs for all times, but in his own way, I believe, he has more than a general lesson to offer for our days, and I have endeavoured to indicate this without, I trust, pointing the moral too obviously.

The two principal lives of St John Vianney are those by Mgr Trochu and Abbé Monnin. Both are very long, the former in its latest French edition running to 718 fair-sized pages, and the latter, in the English edition, to 558 even larger and more closely printed pages. It seemed to me that there was room for a modern life, written for English-speaking readers, and on a less massive scale.

In addition I have made efforts to obtain first-hand accounts of the visits of English-speaking pilgrims to Ars during the lifetime of St John Vianney. Save for that to be found in Ullathorne's printed correspondence I knew of none, but I suspected that there were others recorded in the letters and diaries of the period and that some of these still existed in the archives of monasteries, colleges and convents. I am bound to admit that in spite of advertising and extensive correspondence the harvest of such information has been very small indeed: some of the little that I have discovered appears in the chapter dealing with the pilgrims to Ars. I am convinced, indeed, that there is other evidence of this kind in existence, for it seems improbable that there is no such account extant either in Ireland or the U.S.A., from which, it is known, a number of visitors went to Ars before 1859. Yet in neither country, in spite of widespread inquiries, could I discover any account of even one such visit. I am grateful to the President of Ushaw, Mgr P. Grant, for permission to reproduce, and to Fr D. Milburn for informing me about, the letters of Canon Smith which are quoted in this book; I am grateful also to the Mother Prioress of the Canonesses Regular of the Holy Sepulchre at New Hall for sending to me and allowing me to reproduce the letter from Sister Roskell quoted in the same chapter.

Any biographer of St John Vianney must acknowledge his indebtedness to the long and definitive biography by Mgr Trochu. I used the twelfth French edition: Mgr Francis Trochu, *Le Curé d'Ars: Saint Jean-Marie-Baptiste Vianney* (1786–1859) *d'après toutes les pièces du Procès de Canonisation et de nombreux documents inédits*, Paris and Lyon, no date (the first edition appeared in 1925). For the facts of the life of the Curé d'Ars this is an inexhaustible mine, but the author adopts theories to explain some of his facts (St Philomena, the *Grappin*, for example) that will not stand up to close examination. I have not hesitated to disagree with him when necessary, but am bound to express my grateful acknowledgement to his book, particularly for his establishment of the chronology of the life of the Curé d'Ars, thus correcting Abbé Monnin's work, which still leads students astray over the early years, particularly the period in the seminary, etc. Nevertheless, Abbé Monnin was contemporary with Abbé Vianney and knew him during the last years of his life; his evidence is therefore valuable when he is talking about events within his own experience. I used the English translation: Alfred Monnin, *The Curé of Ars* (*The Blessed Jean-Baptiste-Marie Vianney*), Translation and notes by Bertram Wolferstan, S.J., London, 1924.

A source book that seems to have been neglected by both Mgr Trochu and Abbé Monnin is the *Rituel de Toulon* (the full bibliographical details will be found in the chapter in which it is mentioned); it was from this book that the Curé d'Ars learned most of his theology and it seems surprising that biographers have not laid it under contribution. I am grateful to Dom Aelred Sillem of Quarr Abbey for his trouble in finding a copy of this book for me and enabling me to consult it.

L. C. S.

September 1957

PART I
(1786-1818)

CHAPTER I

EARLY YEARS AND EDUCATION

AT Ars there is a portrait in oils depicting Jean-Marie-Baptiste Vianney as he was towards the end of his life. It shows a face that has become familiar: the long delicate nose with the wide flared nostrils, the large blue eyes looking upwards at you because the head is slightly bowed. The painter has given him a smile that lends an almost roguish air to the face; nevertheless, the long thin line of the mouth is plainly evident, and the expression, as in other portraits, is predominantly sad. There is little flesh on the face, and what there is is deeply furrowed, particularly beneath the cheek-bones. The hair, which is comparatively short on top of the head, hangs down all round it, reaching the nape of the neck and hiding the ears; but it is the nose and the chin, together with the eyes, that are outstanding and give the impression of a beautiful face, the face of a man who has known a fearful struggle which has left its mark on him (despite the lines, there is a transparency about the almost dead-white complexion betokening more than common suffering); but predominantly it is the face of a strong man.

This impression is borne out by the death-bed photograph: although he has lost his teeth, so that the upper lip has fallen back, you can still perceive the straight mouth, finely chiselled nose, prominent chin, which portray the strength of character that must have shone out from his face in life.

It is the portrait of an old man. What did he look like in youth, before suffering, lack of sleep and food, and the other torments which formed the daily background of upwards of forty years had been stamped indelibly on his face? We are told that as a youth his complexion was swarthy and that work in the fields made him very dark. His hair never went completely white. When he was a young man it was dark brown, and the characteristic heart-shaped face with more flesh to deck out the well-defined features must have been that of an attractively handsome man. To the end of his life it was, as it had been in youth, an expressive face: the great mobility of the features endowed with emphasis the simple words that came from his mouth.

For a peasant he was quick-moving, and though deliberate in his actions seemed to be unwilling to waste a moment. Constitutionally he must have been very strong indeed. We shall see how he ill-treated his body for the greater part of his life; that he was able to do so and live to the age of seventy-three, dying in harness, demonstrates the soundness of the peasant stock from which he sprang. He was of less than average height, so that the stoop which developed soon after the age of thirty made him appear small.

To his peasant origins he owed the characteristic simplicity that is to be encountered among many saints of similar upbringing. The peasant farmer of France has long been recognized as the backbone of the country, and the Vianney family is a splendid example of the better type of peasant. Their farm at Dardilly stood in pleasant, well-wooded country in the hills not far from Lyon; from it in an hour or so Lyon could be reached on foot, and looking south from the village can be made out the hill of Fourvières dominating the city, while to the west, on a clear day in autumn, the Forez hills appear bathed in light.

The Vianney family had long held their small farm at Dardilly, with its typical squat homestead, pleasant garden, lawn and outbuildings. Pilgrims who go there nowadays do not see it as it was; it must be visualized without the top storey, which was added in the nineteenth century. In 1770, Pierre Vianney was head of the family.

Tucked away at his farm, and all his interests confined to that rural corner of the Lyonnais, he was unlikely to have heard much of the events which were gradually leading up to the explosion of 1789. He could merely witness some of the results of the social system under which he was able to make a living from his land, and though money was not plentiful, he had food in abundance for his family, shelter and warmth, together with a healthy, happy life, hard work and some security. But he saw the increasing number of beggars who tramped from village to village, the men who had no niche in the social scheme of the times; he did what he could to alleviate their sufferings.

Among them one day in 1770 he entertained St Benedict Joseph Labre, whose enigmatic life can be seen as a protest against the enforced poverty and destitution that afflicted many of his fellow-countrymen. With the others, Benedict was given a bowl of soup and a night's lodging in the barn; unlike the others, some time later he sent a letter of thanks, which was treasured and often spoken about in the family until Pierre Vianney's grandson gave it away to an importunate pilgrim.

On 11 February 1778 Pierre's son Matthieu married Marie Béluse of Ecully; six children were born of this marriage— Catherine, Jean-Marie, François, Jean-Marie, Marguerite, and another François. Catherine married and died young, Jean-Marie lived for only five years, and thus François, as the eldest son, in time became the head of the family and inherited the farm. The second Jean-Marie is the subject of this biography; his sister Marguerite (known familiarly as "Gothon") survived him by nearly twenty years and died at the age of ninety-one; François the younger figures in the early part of this story.

Jean-Marie Vianney was born at midnight on 8 May 1786, and baptized the same day, being called after the brother who had lately died. He was born into a France that was fast passing away, the France of the old order, of the *ancien régime*; as a child he experienced, to the extent that one between the ages of three and fifteen in a rural district could do so, the upheaval of the Revolution, the persecution of religion and proscription of the priesthood. He had his roots, then, in a period which, though just ending, was to exert on him a strong influence that remained for the rest of his days.

He was brought up by parents, he was taught by priests, who belonged to the *ancien régime*. And he was brought up in a countryside where new ideas and movements took long to penetrate. His outlook was coloured by that early training. Examination of the religious situation in France at that period discloses a state of affairs that can best be described as a mixture of faith and formalism —of a Christian tradition living on in men's hearts, and at the same time among many a widespread lip service to the outward observances of religion combined with increasing scepticism. Jean-Marie Vianney had the good fortune to be born in a country district where the Faith was still a living reality, and never encountered the irreligion to be found in Paris or in Lyon.

It would be an over-simplification to see this situation as one of the town as distinct from the country, or of one class of society in comparison with another. Nevertheless, it is true to say that the nobility and the upper classes, in whose ranks were numbered many of the higher clergy, were largely infected with the prevailing scepticism, that the peasants and the country clergy were largely free from it, though some of the country nobility, who were relatively poor, and some of the provincial bishops, who resided in their sees, were untouched by it. Yet even in the country the new ideas were beginning to make their way, but they seem hardly to have penetrated to Dardilly. This generalization—and it is no more than that—of the spirit of the country is illustrated by an example from Cardinal Pacca's *Memoirs*. When he was in Coblenz in 1790 the first batch of French *émigrés* arrived. He describes them as making fun of religion and morality and continuing their intrigues and debauchery as they had done at Versailles. The second party to arrive did not belong to court circles and made an entirely different impression.

Apart from scepticism in certain circles, the formalism that was to be encountered in high places and among some of the inferior clergy is almost to be expected where the State and religion were so inseparably bound up together that the rules of the latter formed part of the laws of the country. In theory, it was possible to be prosecuted for eating meat on a Friday, and though by this time no one thought of invoking the law in this and in similar cases, the fact remained that many things of the sort were so firmly established as customs and traditions that they no longer meant very much. To some the priesthood was a career like any other—the position of country parish priest was not envisaged in that case— and the accumulation of a few benefices—real sinecures—could be the foundation of a fortune.

And there were other causes of weakness in the Church in

France, enemies within the gate who were all the harder to deal with. With the suppression of the Jesuits in 1773 the Jansenists were left with little effective opposition, and even before that date they were powerful enough to sow discord and disorder in many quarters. When, in 1765, the Archbishop of Paris, by the Queen's desire and with the consent of the *Assemblée générale du Clergé*, instituted for the whole of France the feast of the Sacred Heart (already celebrated in several dioceses), the Jansenists, with the help of one or two dissident prelates, stirred up Parliament against the archbishop. The parish priests of Paris supported their archbishop but, when the feast came round, discovered in some cases that their churchwardens had hidden the appropriate vestments. In certain collegiate churches there were quarrels round the lectern at the beginning of Vespers or Matins, some of those present in choir desiring to celebrate the new feast, others intending at all costs to sing the office of the Sunday.

Jansenism, besides opposing the bishops, endeavoured also to attract the inferior clergy by indoctrinating them with the notion that they exercised their spiritual powers under God alone, and were responsible only to him; thus was prepared the way for the Constitutional Church and the Civil Constitution of the Clergy.

The Deist philosophers, Jansenism, Gallicanism, the formalism that is a deadly danger for any institution, all these were enemies with which the Church had to contend. Yet there was a brighter side to the picture. Many country parishes could show a devoted parish priest with a flock that went to church on Sundays and to the sacraments regularly, if somewhat more rarely than we nowadays expect. And though in Lyon, for example, some of the citizens refused to decorate their house for the Corpus Christi procession through the streets, at Dardilly the village was *en fête*. Throughout the eighteenth century, too, side by side with the works of the Encyclopaedists the output of religious literature was large—books of a popular nature for the instruction and improvement of the faithful. The teaching of St Francis de Sales, Louis de Granada, Louis Lallemant and others was spread throughout the country by books adapted for the use of all. Some of the pious literature of the period tried to attract the reader by a catchy title like *La Tabatière mystique* (the mystical snuff box) or *La Purge spirituelle* (the spiritual purge), but in this they were certainly no worse than some examples in the same category in our own day. *The Imitation*, the *Avis et Exercices spirituels* by Suffren, were read and re-read—you can still pick up a much-used, annotated copy of books such as these on the *Quais* in Paris, or on the dusty shelves of some provincial bookseller—and all the classics of the golden age of French mystical and spiritual writing were being reprinted time and again. Years before Dom Guéranger, Nicolas Letourneau produced his Christian Year (*L'Année chrétienne*) in ten volumes, a book which, despite Guéranger's[1] strictures on it, formed generations of Christians, some of whom at the French Revolution proved their mettle.

It was at the end of this period that Jean-Marie Vianney was born. Of his early life at home we are well informed, and if some incidents have been picked out by biographers because they appear to show a precocious piety, they must be seen in perspective against the daily life of the farm with its constant hard labour and the continual struggle against all the difficulties of an agricultural life. He was brought up in a Christian household, one in which it was the custom, as it was in many in those days, to pray together every evening. At the age of eighteen months Jean-Marie, it is recorded, knelt down with the rest, beating his breast at the *Confiteor* and so on. Perhaps it is to this that the breviary refers when it says, *ab infantia plura dedit sanctitatis indicia* ("from infancy he showed many signs of holiness"). To see such signs in the behaviour of very young children is easy enough and usually misleading; frequently they are merely indications of the imitative faculty emerging strongly at a very early age. On the other hand, where children have the opportunity to imitate their elders in such ways they are fortunate in being able at the beginning of their lives to start to form habits which they can recall afterwards not as childish but as grown-up. Children whose prayers are "heard" every night, but never see their parents pray, are less fortunate.

---

[1] Letourneau, in Guéranger's eyes, was unsound on the question of liturgical language and went so far as to translate the Canon of the Mass; that was sufficient to condemn him.

As Jean-Marie grew older he was taught his prayers, the Gospel story and those elements of religion that he was capable of absorbing. In spring and summer the whole family went out to work in the fields, while the youngest children played. Jean-Marie enjoyed his games, and though on occasion he was praised by his mother for being the most obedient of all the children, he was by no means one of those prigs who are sometimes put forward as an example to others; he possessed the impetuosity of the young and the wilfulness that naturally accompanies it.

In the church at Ars there is a fresco showing Marie Vianney discovering her son praying in the cowshed; it is the representation of an event that occurred when Jean-Marie was four. He quietly left the family circle one evening and retired to pray in the stable, kneeling down in a corner. His mother found him at length and reproved him; he promised not to do it again. On another occasion his younger sister, Marguerite, wanted his rosary and the matter nearly came to a tug-of-war between them until their mother intervened and constrained Jean-Marie to give the beads to his sister. Tearfully he obeyed. As a reward he was given a wooden statue of our Lady to which he became even more firmly attached, taking it with him to the fields, setting it up in the house, sleeping with it at night. Often on weekdays he accompanied his mother to an early Mass and so began to gain acquaintance with its external actions. The church-going habit, a growing familiarity with the practice of his religion and a love of it, were due to his mother, who taught him by precept and example from his early years. She was obviously a woman who trained her children carefully, a good wife and mother, beloved of children and husband, but she remains a shadowy figure for us since in all her recorded acts her son obscures her. We know that Jean-Marie held her in esteem and affection and said on more than one occasion that he owed his love of prayer and the Church to her.

Jean-Marie was five in 1791. The events of the previous two years—the taking of the Bastille (1789), the suppression of the monasteries (1790), the seizing of ecclesiastical property—seem to have passed almost unnoticed in the village; presumably tidings of these events penetrated there from Lyon, where they caused some stir. On 14 July 1790, at the primatial church of St John at Lyon, for example, the Chapter was compelled to sing the *Te Deum* to celebrate the anniversary of the taking of the Bastille; the noble canons were rash enough to add Psalm 19, *Exaudiat*, which was usually sung for the king on account of its last verse, *Domine, salvum fac regem* ("Lord, save the King"), but on this occasion the verse was not reached, for when the choir began to sing the previous one, *Ipsi obligati sunt et ceciderunt; nos autem surreximus et erecti sumus* ("they are brought down and fallen; but we are risen and stand upright"), the congregation applauded so heartily that the voices were drowned: the members of the Third Estate were celebrating their victory. Soon afterwards the canons left and the "Constitutional" worship was installed at the cathedral.

The Civil Constitution of the Clergy was voted in 1790 together with the oath of fidelity to it. The choice facing the clergy now, it would seem, was clear; they could choose between the arrangements made for the Church by the Constituent Assembly, which implied separation from Rome but also remaining in their parishes, or they could refuse the oath and, if they could not leave the country, be prepared to suffer more acutely for their convictions.

It all seems clear enough, but to a country parish priest with no opportunity to discuss matters with those who were well informed on all the implications of the Oath, to one for example like Abbé Rey, the parish priest of Dardilly, for all that he was a Doctor of the Sorbonne, the issues were neither so clear-cut nor so simple. In confiscating ecclesiastical property the Assembly had voted an increased stipend for the lesser clergy and to refuse the oath meant losing the small share of what was allotted to them of the booty from the six hundred and fifty-five cathedral and collegiate chapters that had been dissolved. Since for years the parochial clergy had existed on an exceedingly small pittance the increased stipend was a temptation. To leave their parishes meant, in addition, leaving their people uncared for or to the mercies of some stranger; it is not hard to see that, if the oath could be squared somehow with a man's conscience, it would be. Those bishops, the majority, who were strongly opposed to the oath left the country.

Down at Dardilly Dr Rey was not so well placed: he was not a rich man and he lived too far from the frontier to be able to slip over it as some of his colleagues had done. Then, so others of his colleagues told him, it was possible to take the oath with the reservation of remaining in union with Rome—the reservation might even be expressed, but sympathetic churchwardens need not note it in the parish register. Thus all were pleased. Dr Rey swore fidelity to the Civil Constitution of the Clergy and re-mained in his parish.

Things went on as before. Mass was sung on Sundays, the obser-vances of the Christian year came round at their appointed times. Then one day Dr Rey was missing: he had changed his mind and sought the shelter of Lyon with its crowds; from there he managed to find sanctuary in Italy. Although his going was noticed, the new parish priest who came to take his place seemed not to make any changes, though his preaching was unlike Dr Rey's for it was larded with such words as *civisme, citoyen, constitution*; to those in the know this should have been enough. The Vianneys were not in the know, and continued to go to their parish church until one of Marie Vianney's relations from Ecully opened their eyes to the fact that they were sitting under a schismatic.

For the Vianneys, as for all the families who followed their example, began now a period of secret religious practice: Mass in a wood, in a barn, sometimes at their own house, priests in disguise coming out from Lyon or Ecully (which seems to have been a centre for these missionaries), all with a price on their head and the danger of deportation for those caught harbouring them.

Jean-Marie was seven when the Terror came to Lyon and the guillotine was busy all day long. Soldiers of the Convention passed through Dardilly on their way to quell a rising, men came from Lyon to cut down the wayside crosses, the church was closed and the Vianneys were obliged to hide the crucifix which hung from their kitchen wall—all these indications of dark days were not unperceived, obviously, by Jean-Marie, but beyond sharing his parents' anxiety in the vague way that children are aware that something is very much amiss, he was unaffected. The beasts still needed attention, he could still carry his madonna in his pocket, the birds still sang in his father's fields, and, fundamentally, life was happy. But he began to have responsibilities.

At the age of seven a boy could be of some use on the farm and Jean-Marie was entrusted with looking after the beasts. Twice daily he led out the donkey, cattle, and sheep to grass. Generally his sister Gothon went with him. They had to see that the animals did not trespass on their neighbours' ground or on to the growing crops. And in order that they should not be idle their mother had provided them with wool and needles so that they could knit stockings. Jean-Marie told his sister stories from the Bible, and taught her prayers and how to behave at Mass. Sometimes he would ask her to go on with his stocking for him so that he could go and pray in his favourite spot by the stream; there he would set up his wooden statue in a niche scooped out with his hands from the rotting trunk of a willow tree and, kneeling down, say his rosary. Sometimes, having set up a little altar, he would make Gothon play at churches with him, and they would sing what they remembered from the hymns that were sung in the now closed church.

Sometimes other children, looking after their parents' cattle in the nearby fields, would come up to the Vianneys to see what was afoot and were puzzled to know what it was all about; they had forgotten what used to happen at church and probably had not been taught by their parents. Jean-Marie would then turn to preaching, trying to remember what the priest had said at Mass in the woods on the previous Sunday and little bits of catechism that occurred to him. In all this it is difficult to see much more than the ordinary manifestations of childhood, just as it is absurd to take seriously the proposal of marriage that Marion Vincent, the daughter of the Vianneys' neighbours, is said to have made about this time to Jean-Marie. Like him, she was seven years old. It seems strange that writers should point to this incident and his stern refusal of the offer as a sign of his early resolution to remain celibate all his days.

A significant result of the Revolution was to be found in the increasing number of beggars who came to the village. As at all times of social unrest there were those who were the victims of the changes in progress. The traditional Vianney hospitality was not denied to them, and Jean-Marie sometimes helped with their entertainment, or else was sent to take firewood, loaded on the donkey's back, to the poor. Marie Vianney certainly had her hands full, baking every week for her family and frequent guests, and making and repairing clothes, for many garments were given away to the needy, especially to children. Though Jean-Marie never experienced poverty in his childhood, he saw enough of it to realize what it was. Country life, close to nature, tramping to Mass on Sundays through the woods or over the fields to some secret place where a priest was to celebrate, contact with the flotsam of the Revolution, and life in a hard-working family, provided the background to a childhood that was by no means unusual at the time. Of more formal education Jean-Marie received none until the age of nine, save for the first elements of reading taught him by his elder sister Catherine.

The school at Dardilly had been closed as the result of the law which forbade any to teach who had been a member of a religious congregation or a priest or had not taken the oath and acquired a certificate of citizenship. Education was free and obligatory at the age of six. It was easy enough to promulgate the law in Paris: the needs of Dardilly were another matter, and it was only when the shortage of schoolmasters compelled the Government to forget about the oath that a teacher, one Dumas, was found to open a school in the village at the beginning of 1795; since it was winter he did not long want for pupils.

Jean-Marie learnt to read and to write, some simple arithmetic and some elementary notions of history and geography. It is probable that during the summer months the school was closed since all the children would be occupied in the fields. The three winters of 1795, 1796 and 1797 were, it seems, all the schooling that he received until very much later as a young man he had once more to take to his books. From all accounts, in those early years he was diligent and possessed a good memory; that was all that was required for him to profit by those short months of schooling.

In 1797, a priest, M. Groboz, called at the Vianneys' farm. He nquired of Jean-Marie when last he had been to confession.

"But I've never been," was the answer.

"How old are you?"

"Eleven."

"Very well," concluded the priest, "we can remedy that at once."

There and then Jean-Marie went to confession and heard for the first time those words of absolution which in after-life he was to utter more frequently perhaps than any other priest before or since. "I remember it very well," he told people in later years. "It was at home, under our old clock." M. Groboz decided that Jean-Marie should be prepared for his first communion and arranged for him to lodge with his aunt, Marie Humbert, at Ecully, where two nuns, turned out of their convent by the Revolution, worked secretly as catechists.

In May 1798, therefore, he went to Ecully, worked on his uncle's farm and received religious instruction in preparation for his first communion, which he made in 1799. Owing to the difficulties of the time it was a clandestine affair in a manor-house at Ecully. Very early in the morning the children gathered there, while, outside the house, farmers, Matthieu among them, made much of loading and unloading a great wagon of hay which stood in front of the curtained window. Thus they kept watch and did their best to distract attention from the fact that the house seemed to be early astir.

CHAPTER II

THE DAWNING OF A VOCATION

AT the age of thirteen, having made his first communion and finished the scanty schooling that was judged necessary for him, Jean-Marie began to work on the farm in real earnest. His days were filled with the hard physical toil that would increasingly be his lot for the rest of his days. The vines must be tended, the art of ploughing mastered, the whole craft of farming learned thoroughly. It was an arduous life that stretched out before him, but one with many compensations to offset the hard work, the disappointments, the struggle against the various hazards that nature seems to hold in store for those who farm. Now in adolescence he began to show more clearly his attraction for the things of religion. He was naturally devout and gave what time he could to prayer. He made a practice of praying at his work, of offering his work as a prayer, he read the lives of the saints, the *Imitation* and the Gospels. At night in the corner of the stable loft, where he slept with his elder brother François, he lit a candle and read his few books, sometimes to the latter's annoyance. His mother finally told him that he must take all the sleep that he could.

To his great joy he was able to go to church. With the advent of Bonaparte, though the laws relating to religion were not at once repealed, in practice a certain tolerance made things much easier. Abbé Groboz and Abbé Balley began to say Mass publicly at Ecully and there the Vianney family went every Sunday. With the signing of the Concordat in July 1801, and its ratification in April 1802, the Church in France emerged definitively from the catacombs. At Dardilly this event was anticipated by some months. Abbé Rey had returned to his parish as soon as he could and in 1802 the worship of the Church was restored to the village and was celebrated as it had been in times past. Jean-Marie made a habit of going to church, whenever possible, before beginning his day's work. In the summer he had to be early in the fields and could only obey the summons of the church bell, as it rang for the elevation, by praying as he continued his labours. On Sundays he was up early and spent much time in church. Certainly by this time he felt sure that he was called to the priesthood, but he could not be blind to the fact that there were great difficulties in the way.

To begin with there was his lack of learning. His French was that of a peasant, and in addition it would be necessary to know Latin. Then, too, it was hard to see how his father could spare him from the farm and, if he were able to do so, find the money required for the training for the priesthood. François, his elder brother, was approaching military age, and, if he had the misfortune to be called to the colours, his father would have to let him go or find the money to pay a substitute (the customary price at that time was £120 to £140). Catherine was engaged to be married and would soon require a dowry. It hardly seemed possible that his father would be in a position to pay the seminary fees.

His mother and his aunt, whom he informed of his longing, were entirely on his side, and though they appreciated the difficulties as well, probably better, than he did, being practical women they endeavoured to see a way round them: it was not certain that François would draw a number requiring him to suffer conscription, and Catherine's dowry was surely not so heavy as to strain resources to the utmost. The two women, talking it over, were impressed by Jean-Marie's reasons: he was impelled by the loftiest motives. The dawn of an authentic priestly vocation is sometimes manifested by certain signs among which can be discerned an element of self. Thus a young man may be attracted by the idea of performing the ceremonies of the Church, by the privilege of saying Mass and so on. This is a partly, sometimes a purely, human attraction. If accompanied by other signs, which are easy to recognize, such vocations may well be genuine. Of Jean-Marie's vocation on close examination there could be no doubt. His predominant motive was selfless; he wanted to be a priest for the glory of God and the good of souls. Increasingly he realized the dearth of priests; perhaps he saw neighbouring villages without a pastor, or heard Abbé Rey preaching about it or reading a pastoral letter from Cardinal Fesch on the subject. "If I were a priest," said Jean-Marie, "I should try to save many souls."

Though his mother not only approved his intention but gladly welcomed it, there still remained Matthieu Vianney to be tackled. It would not do to blurt it out: the proper occasion must be chosen. A little time went by before Jean-Marie approached him, and then, by ill-fortune, he chose entirely the wrong moment; he cannot have known that news had just been received that François had been unlucky in the draw and must serve in the army or pay someone to go in his place. Matthieu, reeling under this blow to his pocket and with Catherine's dowry still rankling in his mind, would not consider the idea for an instant. In any case, he urged, a priest's was no life to hanker after at that time—and who knew whether things would not suddenly be as bad or even worse again? Besides, Jean-Marie was close on eighteen: where was he to find anyone to teach him even the rudiments of Latin and all the rest that he must know before a seminary would take him? In any case, he ended the discussion without further ado, he needed his son's work on the farm now that he was of an age to be of some use.

Matthieu Vianney probably knew his financial resources to the last halfpenny and spoke with full knowledge of the difficulties in Jean-Marie's way, though he probably exaggerated the amount of learning required to enter the seminary: like all those whose knowledge is confined to a trade that is unbookish he was impressed by any evidence of learning, however small. No doubt he credited the clergy with immense stores of knowledge and vast learning; he would have been surprised to know that great numbers of them were neither learned nor anxious to be so.

For two years Matthieu held out. Jean-Marie said no more, but it is probable that his mother did, and during that time his father must often have heard what an exemplary son he possessed, how obvious it was that he should be a priest and what an honour it would be for the family. Abbé Rey, too, must have known something of all this at the beginning, but was unable to do anything much about it for in 1803 he resigned his benefice and sought in Lyon his well-earned retirement; save for the short break at the

Revolution he had been parish priest of Dardilly since February 1753, a period of fifty years. He enjoyed his rest for a year only, dying in 1804.

At about this time occurred another change in the diocese which proved of great benefit to Jean-Marie. Abbé Charles Balley, a former canon regular of St Geneviève, was appointed parish priest of Ecully. He was a man in his middle fifties who during the Terror had laboured to keep the Faith alive in the Lyonnais countryside, and already the Vianney family had encountered him when his missionary expeditions brought him to Dardilly or its neighbourhood. In his new parish he set about his task of reviving the religious life of the countryside, endeavouring to repair some of the damage of the Revolution. With the encouragement of the diocesan authority he sought out likely subjects as recruits for the depleted ranks of the diocesan clergy, and to ensure their preliminary education established in his presbytery a small school where these lads could obtain the elementary knowledge of Latin and other subjects needed for entrance to the seminary.

On hearing this news Jean-Marie's hopes revived. His mother explained to Matthieu that it would not mean a great expense to send Jean-Marie to Ecully. He could lodge with his relations and go to Abbé Balley for his lessons. Matthieu, faced with this new scheme, and observing his son's persisting desire, withdrew his opposition. Jean-Marie was free to go to Ecully. Marie Vianney and her sister Marguerite Humbert sought out Abbé Balley and informed him of all the details of Jean-Marie's case. Their journey was fruitless: Abbé Balley could find no room for him. As a last resort they sent Catherine's husband (M. Melin) to plead Jean-Marie's case. Abbé Balley was persuaded to see him and, having interviewed him and questioned him at length about his vocation, consented to find room for him.

Jean-Marie was in his twentieth year when he went back to school to endeavour to learn what most boys, if they are to know it at all, should acquire by the age of ten. The elements of French grammar needed to be learned afresh for what he had obtained from M. Dumas's teaching at Dardilly had through disuse practically gone from his memory. When at last he tackled his Latin grammar and syntax he discovered that the memory of an adult was by no means that of a child; it was extremely difficult to get even the declension of *rosa* or the conjugation of *amo* by heart. In addition, it must be confessed, he gives no evidence of being very bright. On the contrary. And for some years, working on his father's farm, his thinking had been of an entirely different kind; generally speaking his intellect had lain fallow for too long. He set to work with a will, however, bearing the sniggers of his fellow pupils, all of them much younger than he, as he struggled to master the simplest rules of syntax or to construe Erasmus's Latin reader of selected stories from the Old Testament (*Selectae e Veteri Testamento historiae ex Erasmi paraphrasibus excerptae*). He prayed constantly and did penance to win the favour of heavenly help with his studies. He fasted continually, helped the poor from his meagre resources, and on one occasion went so far as to give away his boots when, on his way home to Dardilly for the afternoon, he encountered a beggar. Despite his efforts lasting over several months he made practically no progress and the signs of his interior conflict began to show themselves in his now haggard face. Abbé Balley spoke to him, enjoining moderation in penance, and endeavouring to encourage him.

Jean-Marie revealed that he felt that his efforts were useless and that he would do better to return home to his father's farm and the work of the fields; that, he knew, was within his grasp. It was a temptation that Abbé Balley, who was convinced of his vocation, found some difficulty in repelling; his pupil seemed at the the end of his tether. Finally, to postpone an irrevocable decision —once Jean-Marie returned home it was obvious that Matthieu would not let him go again—and to give the young man a change of scene and, if not a rest, a holiday from Latin, Abbé Balley proposed that he should go on a pilgrimage to the shrine of St John Francis Regis at Louvesc.

Jean-Marie seized on the idea with enthusiasm: he would go on foot, begging his bread *en route*. That the shrine was some sixty-five miles away in the mountains of Vivarais did not deter him. He arrived there exhausted, having failed to find a night's

lodging or a charitable soul to give him anything to eat. The few
francs he had brought with him he preserved intact, keeping his
vow to beg. At Louvesc he prayed at the saint's tomb with the
thought in mind that St John Francis Regis, who at the price of
great hardship and suffering had evangelized this mountainous
country in the seventeenth century, and prevented the spread of
Protestantism, would help him to become a priest and save souls
in the countryside of Lyonnais. The priest who heard his confession insisted on his buying food on the way home: when he
arrived, he advised him, he could give alms to the poor.

On his return to Ecully his progress in Latin, though by no
means spectacular, was sufficiently improved to give him at least
hope that he would finally acquire enough to begin his philosophy and theology. He probably did not realize, though Abbé
Balley certainly did, how low was the standard required at that
time and how far short of even that Jean-Marie was and seemed
likely to remain. Nevertheless, there now seemed a glimmer of
hope that he might just scrape through.

One difficulty surmounted seemed to lead only to another: his
military service loomed ahead. Napoleon's campaigns, brilliantly
successful as they were, proved costly in manpower; young men
were being called up before their time, and there was some danger
that Jean-Marie would have to go even before 1807 when his turn
came round. Cardinal Fesch, Archbishop of Lyon, had managed
to obtain exemption for his seminarists, and Abbé Balley contrived
to avert the danger by having Jean-Marie's name put down as an
ecclesiastical student. For the time being, at least, he seemed to be
safe.

It was in 1807 that Jean-Marie, together with his sister Gothon,
was confirmed by Cardinal Fesch in the parish church of Ecully.
In his heavy coach, "Uncle Fesch", as he was familiarly known
on account of his relationship to Napoleon, trundled round his
diocese in all winds and weathers carrying out the visitation of the
parishes and administering confirmation to the many who had
been unable to receive this sacrament in the past decade. At his
confirmation Jean-Marie took the name of Baptiste, which
thereafter he added to his signature.

Life went on quietly for another couple of years and Jean-Marie continued to struggle with his Latin. He helped Abbé Balley, seeing to the garden and working as sacristan. In a year or two he could look forward to entering the diocesan seminary and beginning his professional training for the priesthood. After that one crisis of his vocation, before his pilgrimage to Louvesc, he seems no more to have been troubled about his future, until at this time fell the blow which appeared to postpone, possibly for years, the realization of his hopes: calling-up papers in the name of Jean-Marie Vianney were served on him at Dardilly.

All sorts of conjectures have been made to account for this episode in Jean-Marie's career. Possibly Abbé Balley forgot to send in his pupil's name a second time and the officials, failing to find it in the list for 1809, concluded that the J.-M. Vianney who figured in the 1807 list had left the seminary. Legally, in any case, exemption applied to those in major orders, and the seminarists of Lyon enjoyed it as a special concession obtained by Cardinal Fesch from his nephew, and after all, Jean-Marie was not strictly speaking a seminarist. Relations between "Uncle Fesch" and his nephew had their ups and downs; when they were strained Napoleon was quite capable of withdrawing all concessions, and in addition at this time he was in urgent need of men.

Not without difficulty Matthieu Vianney was persuaded to put up the £140 or so required to pay for a substitute, but no one could be found to accept the proposition; Jean-Marie had no option but to go.

It was, he felt, the end of any hope of becoming a priest. The long years that he would be away—he might well be thirty on his return—and the considerable time that he would require after that for his philosophy and theology, seemed to postpone the priesthood to a future so shadowy and distant as to deprive it of all reality. Nor was he unaware that the chances of returning at all were not entirely favourable.

The nature of military service in those days, conditions in Napoleon's army, Jean-Marie's educational needs and all the special circumstances of his case made it a real hardship for him to join the army. Under modern conditions it is a debatable point

whether the relatively short period of compulsory military training that is imposed in many countries today should be regarded as
something to be avoided at all costs by clerical students. There
are many obvious disadvantages about the system of national
service, but they apply to all young men who are obliged to undergo it. In its favour must be mentioned the fact that not infre-
quently it serves to mature the young conscript who, entering as
a boy, emerges with at least the makings of a man. It can be regarded perhaps as a necessary evil, but it is not necessarily to the
clerical student's advantage that he avoids it. As a priest he will
have to share the life of his people and to deal with their hopes
and difficulties, joys and sorrows: if he has not shared an experience that is now part of almost every young man's life he is at
more than a little disadvantage.

For Jean-Marie, as it turned out, his military service did not
amount to much. On 26 October he reported at the barracks at
Lyon. One whole day was sufficient to show him that military life
was even worse than he feared. He was, we are told, profoundly
shocked by all that he saw and heard. On 28 October he was too
ill to get up in the morning and the doctor ordered his transfer
to hospital.

It has been said that his mortifications combined with his hard
studying and this sudden change in his way of life were responsible
for his illness. Yet he had experienced but one whole day of barrack
life and before that showed no signs of delicate health. The cause
of his illness, I believe, is to be found in the great disappointment
he suffered in having to postpone all hope of ordination and the
severe psychological shock administered by that short encounter
with other recruits, most of them, probably, men who were
serving because they had been paid to take the place of others.
Jean-Marie had so far led a sheltered life, his experience of the
world was very small and his delicacy of feeling, and of conscience,
extreme. His whole being reacted violently in revulsion, and as a
consequence he was found on the morning of 28 October in
high fever.

For a fortnight he was in the military hospital at Lyon. His
parents and friends visited him there. He spoke, says his cousin

Marguerite Humbert, almost entirely of God and of the need to do his will. A fortnight later (12 November) he was well enough to get up, but still sufficiently weak not to march with the rest of his contingent to Roanne for training before setting out for Spain. He followed behind in a cart, but the journey was too much for him; he was sent to hospital on arrival and there remained six weeks, petted by the nuns who made much of him. Here once again his parents came to see him and finally took leave of him with little expectation of seeing him again: they thought that he would die on the journey to Spain, or that if he arrived there he would be killed in battle.

On 5 January 1810 he was told that he must join a detachment setting out on the long march to the Spanish frontier; in the course of that afternoon he was to call at the adjutant's office for his marching orders. Jean-Marie left the hospital to go to the office, but spying a church on his way and with ten minutes to spare went in to pray. "There," he related, "all my troubles melted away like snow in the sunshine." On arrival at the office he found it closed.

On 6 January he got ready for the journey, took leave of the nuns and set out for the adjutant's office once more. There he learned that the contingent had left without awaiting him and was told in no uncertain terms what was the official view of his conduct. He was likely to be arrested as a deserter. However, they were kind to him: he was given his route and told to catch up the rearguard.

He started off along the road to Clermont. On he tramped through Villemontais where the road begins to rise towards the mountainous Forez region. He was very tired, and the savage beauty of the countryside meant nothing to him as he trudged along in the teeth of a biting wind. Above all, he wanted rest and food, so that a few hours before nightfall, at the sight of a small copse a hundred yards or so off his path, he made for it over a ploughed field. He sat there saying his rosary, the picture, one imagines, of misery. A young man came up and questioned him. Jean-Marie revealed his plight. Then the stranger, taking the tired conscript's pack on his own shoulders, told him to follow.

For some time they scrambled in the darkness along a mountain track, climbing over boulders, crossing a torrent, making for the forest of Madelaine. Jean-Marie's guide, whose named turned out to be Guy, questioned him as they struggled along. The young recruit told him the whole story.

"I must say," remarked Guy, "you don't look much like a soldier."

He went on to say that Jean-Marie would be safe enough in the well-wooded mountains. There were other deserters there.

"In fact," he concluded, "I'm one myself."

Jean-Marie protested. He had to obey orders, and his parents would be in serious trouble if he deserted. In view of subsequent events, it can only be supposed that his protest was very half-hearted, but he was at the end of his tether and must not be judged too severely; all he could hope for, or think of, just then, was shelter for the night and food to eat.

When they had climbed to a height of two thousand feet leaving, a few hundred feet below them, the village of Noës, a small pocket of human habitation in the immense expanse of trees covering the mountainside, they obtained lodging in a clog-maker's hut. The man and his wife offered the two young men a crust of bread and gave up to them the only bed in the hut.

The next morning Guy led his new-found friend to one Claude Tornaire, who took on the pair of them sawing wood for a couple of days. At the end of that time Jean-Marie was asked to find work elsewhere. He went to Pont, hoping to secure the position of schoolmaster, but was unlucky. One had just then been appointed.

He now bethought him, somewhat tardily, of the Mayor of Noës, whose duty it was, in virtue of his office, to help him on his way with all possible speed in pursuit of his regiment. M. Paul Fayot, the mayor, lived a mile and a quarter away, up the mountains in a hamlet called Robins. He was not best pleased to see Jean-Marie; already he was hiding two deserters in his outhouse and if the provost-marshal's men came poking about it might go badly with him. But he was kind-hearted and made what arrangements he could for Jean-Marie's safety, obtaining lodging for

him in the house opposite with his cousin, the widow Claudine
Fayot. Jean-Marie was taken in there and kept hidden during the
day; after dark he was allowed to join the family. Under the name
of Jerome Vincent he thus spent the next two years at Robins.
The hamlet was well placed to observe the approach of the
military in search of deserters and there was little danger of
surprise. In any case they called first on the mayor, who could be
relied upon to reassure them and deflect them from seeking in
places where they would be unwelcome.

*   *   *

This is a strange episode in Jean-Marie's career. What are we to
make of it? In after-life he made no secret of it and never looked
back on it as discreditable. The fact that to all intents and purposes
he deserted cannot be called in question, though desertion at that
particular period was by no means the same thing as nowadays.
Napoleon's constant call for men and more men to fill the gaps in
his fighting forces was made to a population that was accustomed
to the idea of a professional army or to fighting when the country
was in peril. The levy on the nation's manhood, taken unscru-
pulously, persisting over a long period, and all to satisfy the ambition of one man, was not only unpopular, it was held in con-
tempt, and those who could avoid serving with the army did so
with a good conscience. This was a state of mind that was particularly prevalent among the peasants. Yet the fact remains that Jean-
Marie deserted with full knowledge of the consequences that
would be felt more acutely by his parents than by himself. That
side of his conduct can hardly be defended, but examination of the
events leading up to it may possibly throw light on his state of
mind at the time. During his illness at Lyon he was talking to his
cousin about the will of God, and one cannot escape the impression
that he did so because he had it very much on his mind that it was
going to be difficult for him to do what he thought to be his duty.
The illness whose onset occurred almost immediately on his
joining up looks uncommonly like the coming into operation of
a defence mechanism in the face of disagreeable circumstances.

Nowadays we should probably say that he suffered a nervous breakdown. When at Roanne in church all his "difficulties melted away like snow in the sunshine" it may well have been an unconscious refusal to go to the office to pick up his papers—an experience that happens to many people. We are asked to do something that is unpleasant to us. Intending to do it we postpone it and as likely as not forget it. Jean-Marie, busy with his prayers in the church, forgot temporarily the unpleasant duty awaiting him, and arrived too late at the office. On his way to join his unit he turns away from the road to rest, he hangs about for two days with Guy, and though protesting that he will not desert, effectively does so, takes a job, saws wood, tries to become a schoolmaster. Only then does he think of the mayor, and the latter, when eventually he is run to earth, turns out to have his own private interpretation of the law; he tells Jean-Marie that in virtue of his office of mayor he relieves him of the obligation of military service. That the deserter must still remain in hiding should have struck him as strange.

It is probable that the mayor, a man of independent mind, like many mountain folk, and a confirmed opponent of Napoleon's military schemes and his arrangements for filling the depleted ranks of his army, when faced with the scruples of the anxious, and apparently conscious-stricken youth, told him that he would be safe enough up there in the mountains.

"But I shall be a deserter," Jean-Marie insisted.

"Oh, I'm mayor," came the ready answer. "I'll look after you. Why, I can dispense you from serving with the army."

Such a remark, made jokingly, was either taken seriously—which would seem to display a *naïveté* almost too extreme to be true—or else seized upon as an excuse to insist no further. Jean-Marie, in other words, had heard what he wanted to hear. His whole conduct, from the time of his joining up until his desertion became effective, seems to portray a young man in the throes of a conflict, trying to resolve it by accepting what was an unpleasant duty, yet unconsciously seeking from it an escape which he found eventually in the mountain fastness at Noës.

It is no denigration of Jean-Marie to interpret his actions in this way. All his biographers, faced with his equivocal conduct on this occasion, have sought to justify it, one seeing his avoidance of soldiering in Spain as a miracle; we need not go so far. His character was sound enough and his conscience was clear, but his mind was set on ordination, he was conscious that he was called by God to the priesthood. When out of the blue came the call to the army, together with the psychological shock of the sudden dashing of all his hopes and of his one day among his fellow-conscripts in the barrack-room, followed quickly by the weakness resulting from his illness, and the half-hearted attempt to rejoin his unit, he was presented with a trial too heavy for him to bear, a conflict so severe that, with a knowledge of all the facts, the general lines of its resolution might have been foreseen.

Such an explanation fits in with the evidence about this episode given for the beatification: a witness well acquainted with the circumstances declared concerning the Noës episode that Jean-Marie's disobedience was more apparent than real and the fact that "he did not rejoin his regiment was due to unforeseen circumstances rather than to a preconceived plan". That a contributory factor to the unforeseen circumstances was an unconscious motivation which caused Jean-Marie to desert when the opportunity offered is in accordance with the facts and offers an explanation of his conduct that does not strain them.

*   *   *

For two years, under the name of Jerome Vincent, Jean-Marie remained at Robins, where he quickly became a favourite with his hostess and her family. His days were spent in the stables, and only when it was dark did he venture out. During the long winter evenings he passed the time in the kitchen with the family, reading the Gospel to them, telling them stories from the lives of the saints. He taught the little Fayots reading, writing and the catechism. Down at Noës the church bell rang in the mornings for Mass, but it was some time before Jean-Marie dared venture out. On Sundays he was left at home with little Claudine, aged three, and as Mass went on in the church he told her what was happening,

making her kneel and sit in accordance with the different parts
of the Mass, teaching her what the bell at the elevation meant and
so on. As the snow gradually disappeared with the spring sunshine, and the forest paths became passable once more, patrols
began to make their way up to Noës and beyond. On three
occasions they called at Madame Fayot's but found nothing since
Jean-Marie was working in the woods. Once they came when he
was in a field near the house. The agreed signal was given and
Jean-Marie slipped quickly into the stable and was up through the
hole in the planks and into the loft without being observed. He
buried himself in the hay and lay there in the great heat (the hay
was fermenting), terrified lest he should sneeze, afraid for his own
skin and even more for those who had given him shelter. The
soldiers conducted a perfunctory search of the stables, and then
proceeded to the loft, where they were more painstaking, poking
about in the hay and running their swords through it. Jean-Marie
received a flesh wound which though not serious was extremely
painful; he managed to keep quiet and at last the troop made off
to drink with the mayor before going down to the valley again.
A little longer and Jean-Marie might well have suffocated. Many
years afterwards, recounting the incident, he said that he had never
suffered so much in all his life as on that occasion, and that he
promised God that never afterwards would he complain. This
promise he kept.

Somewhat tardily, we may think, he began to be worried about
what had happened to his parents as a result of his desertion. He
could not obtain news of them until Claudine Fayot, urged by
the village doctor to take the waters at Charbonnières-les-Bains,
near Lyon, consented to do so and set off armed with a letter from
Jean-Marie for his parents. Until she showed the letter Madame
Fayot was none too well received by the Vianney family. Directly
Marie Vianney had read it, however, she was overjoyed.
Matthieu's reaction was in character too. "Tell me where he is,"
he cried, "I'll soon get him back!" He had lost a good farm-hand
to the Church, and was now smarting under the fines inflicted on
him on account of Jean-Marie's desertion. Madame Claudine
stood up to Matthieu. "If you find out where I live," she said,

"you still won't find your son; I shall hide him elsewhere. He is worth far more than any of your money."

Jean-Marie was glad to have news of his family, but was sorry to hear of their difficulties on his account. Towards the middle of September 1810 he managed to send for his books to Ecully whence they were brought by Madame Bibost, a widow who lived next door to the presbytery. A month later she was at Robins again, bearing news that was more welcome than the Latin grammar: as a result of the amnesty granted by Napoleon on the occasion of his marriage to Marie-Louise of Austria, Jean-Marie was free to return to Dardilly; provided he could furnish a substitute he would not be called upon to serve with the army. Matters were soon arranged. Jean-Marie's younger brother François agreed to go in his place on condition that he received three thousand francs (£120) out of Jean-Marie's share of the father's estate.

A pleasant side to this unhappy episode is provided by the sorrow of the people of Robins and Noës at Jerome Vincent's departure. They showed their esteem for him by presents which were intended to be of some help to him on his way to the priesthood. A cassock was made for him, Madame Claudine Fayot gave him linen to use in his presbytery when he should occupy one, an old peasant women sold a pig and gave him the thirty francs she received from the sale. The truth is that Jean-Marie was a good young man, an attractive personality, and was beginning to exert that influence and display those winning ways that in after-life emerged as a prominent characteristic. At this time he was not a saint but his feet were set on the path towards becoming one; holiness has a way of producing attractive personalities; indeed it would be odd if it did not do so, since it is a perfecting of the whole man.

CHAPTER III

STEPS TO THE PRIESTHOOD

AT the beginning of January 1811 Jean-Marie made the journey back to Dardilly. His joy at returning home was matched by his mother's at seeing him again and by his father's at the departure of the bailiffs whom, by reason of Jean-Marie's desertion, he had been obliged to lodge and feed; he may well have thought that his son's sojourn in the mountains, and the rougher life that he led there, might have put all ideas of the priesthood out of mind and given a taste for farm life once more. Although François the eldest worked hard, Jean-Marie's pair of hands were still urgently needed, the more so since Napoleon's army had now taken François the youngest.

In January there was little enough to do on the farm. Jean-Marie was able to visit his old haunts, the stream, the fields in which he played and worked as a boy. The happiness at his return home was marred in some degree by his mother's frail appearance; she no longer seemed the active woman that he had left behind and she sought her armchair by the hearth as often as she could, leaving Gothon to look after the cooking and housework. Soon afterwards Marie Vianney took to her bed and it became obvious that she had not long to live. Before Easter she was dead.

Jean-Marie lost his mother at a time when he still needed her help towards his goal, and that help she provided until almost her last breath, extracting from her husband on her deathbed a promise that he would place no further obstacle in his son's way. Thus it was, as he still freshly mourned her, that Jean-Marie returned to Ecully and his studies, comforted by the thought that up to the last she believed in his vocation and had helped him on his road. He was conscious of what he owed to her and he never forgot it to the end of his days.

Latin grammar came no more easily for having been neglected for many months and time was getting on. Abbé Balley decided that Jean-Marie must now take the first step, receive the tonsure, wear the cassock, and become, in fact, a cleric. The pupil was now living in the presbytery with his master and outside his periods of study helping him in various ways.

Presbytery life under the régime in force at Ecully was probably more uncomfortable than in others at that time. Abbé Balley, then just over sixty, was an austere if kind master; he led a penitential life, preserving some of the practices of his youth as a canon regular, and inspired his pupil with similar notions.

It was usual in the diocese of Lyon, as no doubt elsewhere in France at that time, for those in the junior seminaries to receive the tonsure at the beginning of their year in rhetoric, that is, as we should say in this country, on entering the sixth form at school. Abbé Balley received permission to present his pupil and Jean-Marie was tonsured on 28 May 1811. He had just passed his twenty-fifth birthday when technically he became a churchman and began to wear the cassock, the black sash and the *rabat* (or bands) which formed the obligatory costume of the clergy. Henceforward as an ecclesiastic he had the right to the title of Abbé, and so he was known for the rest of his life; Abbé Vianney he now becomes for the remainder of this biography.

Madame Bibost, the good friend who made the forty-mile journey from Ecully to Robins with his Latin grammar and other books the previous year, looked after his clothes for him, her interest in his progress and general well-being the greater because her own son too was a seminarist. With study and work in the garden, prayer and reading the lives of the saints, serving Mass every morning for his tutor, who was an object lesson to the young man of what a priest should be, tramping the country lanes in all winds and weather on visits to the sick and, when the Eucharist was taken, carrying the candle and ringing the bell, sometimes after dinner passing a quiet half-hour with *Mère* Bibost by way of recreation, there thus passed a whole year of what can only be called Abbé Vianney's practical apprenticeship to the priesthood.

There are worse ways of preparing for a calling than by living in daily contact with a man who is exercising it devotedly. Abbé Balley saw clearly, however, that the time had come for his pupil to have more regular technical training, for what was offered in the seminary at that time can hardly be called more than that. It would certainly be wrong to speak of it as anything else, as it would be wrong to call the modern seminary course, twice as long though it is, education. Abbé Vianney was faced with a three-year course to be undergone before ordination, one year of philosophy and two of theology. It is possible that he faced it not without a certain trepidation and not without the feeling, in addition, that it represented a three-year test of endurance. His vocation in reality required no trial, but he was in need of the elementary notions of theology that, it appeared, were only to be obtained in the seminary. Abbé Balley, who had been at one point in his career a seminary professor, knew what was in store for his pupil and what advantages he could derive from such a life. Principally he would come into contact with others, his future colleagues in the ministry; some of his "corners" would be rubbed off in the process, and he would obtain the minimum of knowledge required for ordination.

At the beginning of November 1812 Abbé Vianney set out for Verrières, where the year of philosophy was taught. What at that time formed practically an annexe to the major seminary at Lyon had begun as a presbytery school for a few aspirants to the priesthood like Abbé Balley's establishment at Ecully. It now housed, though that is hardly an adequate description, two hundred or so pupils, who were divided between two classes. Abbé Vianney, assigned to that taught by Abbé Chezelles, was not only the senior student but older than his professor by a couple of years. He did not take kindly to philosophy; he found the teaching method in use difficult to follow. The professor dictated in class his explanation of the text-book—a Latin manual of Cartesian inspiration—and questioned his pupils in Latin. Abbé Vianney found it difficult enough to make out the meaning of the text-book, laboriously translating it line by line and puzzling over the French sentences thus evolved. To the professor's questions he could make no answer; he understood not a word of what they were about.

The youths who were his classmates looked forward to these exhibitions as a diversion, but their enjoyment of them did not last long. Half a dozen others in the class were experiencing a similar difficulty and after a month or so the seven of them were formed into a small class which was taught in French. This was some advantage, though it meant that when they came to their theology they would discover that the Latin difficulty had only been shelved not solved.

At Verrières Abbé Vianney certainly suffered both from the difficulties that he encountered in his studies and from his fellow-students. There was something like ten years difference between him and most of them; he had to endure their humour, or what passed for it, and it is possible that they did not display that serious-ness of demeanour and purpose that was habitual with him. He was not, however, the only student of riper years. In class with him, suffering the same indignity of having to be taught in French, was a young man of twenty-three, Abbé Marcellin Champagnat, who had begun the study of Latin at the age of seventeen. Like Abbé Vianney, he too had made the pilgrimage to Louvesc, and for the same reason, and had there found encouragement to persevere. The two young men were drawn together by their common purpose and the similar nature of the difficulties with which they had to contend. Abbé Champagnat was to carve out his own niche in the history of the Church; he founded the Little Brothers of Mary, usually known as the Marist brothers, to teach in elementary and agricultural schools, orphanages and deaf and dumb asylums (they now number upwards of ten thousand members and are to be found all over the world) and he was beatified in 1955.

The year at Verrières was soon over, and beyond a short and not very pleasant taste of community life it cannot be said that Abbé Vianney gained very much from it. Abbé Balley, perusing his report at the end of the year, noted with pleasure that his charge's conduct, character and application were all classed as good, but that unfortunately his grasp of the elementary philosophy that he had been studying was exceedingly weak.

In fact, Verrières was a year wasted. In July 1813 he was back at Ecully for the summer holidays and Abbé Balley took him in hand for the approaching two years at the major seminary in Lyon. It is not without interest to note, as Mgr Trochu points out, that these were the last holidays that Abbé Vianney was ever to take.

The major seminary of St Irenaeus at Lyon was under the direction of secular priests, replacing the Sulpicians, who, as a result of the imperial decree of 1811, had been forbidden to teach in the seminaries of France. The new professors endeavoured to continue the traditions established by their predecessors, teaching dogma, scripture, liturgy, canon law and moral theology and doing their best to produce virtuous and well-informed priests. The whole course had to be crammed into two years, so that the notions imparted of some of the subjects were no doubt sketchy, but they were sufficient to enable a man to minister to a parish, to say Mass and hear confessions. Cardinal Fesch, who took a great interest in his seminary, was obliged to be content with a relatively low standard. Hardly had the seminarists completed two or three years of theology, writes his biographer, than he ordained them and sent them out to the parishes; on one point only was he exacting: their piety was to be above reproach. Providing that they knew enough to deal with ordinary cases in the confessional and had the sense to ask advice in particularly difficult ones, he was satisfied. He looked forward to the time when his seminarists would have a four-year course, but his need of priests was so great that he could not spare them the time at that period.

Abbé Vianney found at the seminary some of his fellow-students of Verrières, among them Marcellin Champagnat; he shared a room with three others and gave, we are told, an example of regularity and observance of the rule that was outstanding. But there was nothing extraordinary in his conduct nor, unfortunately, his studies, save that he could make no progress at all. The classes in Latin, the dictated notes and the rapid questions in the same language, were entirely beyond him. He found it difficult enough to translate the manual in use, Bailly's *Theologia dogmatica et moralis ad usum seminariorum*. It is no more difficult than the usual theological manual, once the jargon has been mastered, and it can only be inferred that Abbé Vianney's Latin, for all his efforts, was very weak indeed. Finally, the professor appointed one of the leading students, Abbé Jean Duplay, to be Vianney's private tutor. When things were explained to him in French he managed to follow them and to answer questions intelligently. One of the professors also took pity on him and gave him a few lessons from a book written in French, the *Rituel de Toulon*; not exactly a handy compendium, it was in three stout quarto volumes, but the busy parish priest's "inquire within upon everything", written, it would seem, for just such a one as this seminarist of twenty-seven. It was one thing to enjoy these aids to learning, it was another to exhibit the fruits of his study to the examiners towards the end of the scholastic year. The questions were in Latin, the examining board, with two hundred and fifty young men to interrogate, could waste no time; seeing that he could answer no question put to him and was, so far as they could gather, utterly unacquainted with the subject-matter of his course, they had no option. They informed him that it would be useless for him to return after the holidays.

He returned to Ecully heartbroken. Far more than his other disappointments this one seems to have affected him the most. He felt that it was indeed the end of all his hopes. He even made up his mind that if he could not be a priest he would become a Christian Brother and went to call at their establishment in Lyon before setting off for Ecully. There he arranged to join their noviciate in a few days' time.

Abbé Balley received him with his usual affection and heard his tale of woe. But he would have none of his new project of becoming a Christian Brother. He told Abbé Vianney to write off at once to the noviciate and cancel his application, and, having infused a little confidence into his pupil, rushed off to Lyon to arrange matters.

Once more at Ecully, thanks to Abbé Balley's negotiations, Abbé Vianney sat down to study. This time it was not Latin. The three volumes of the *Rituel de Toulon* were once more called into service and with Abbé Balley's explanations they proved to be not too hard to master. Indeed, from subsequent events, we can gather that they were learned thoroughly, in those parts at least which applied to the functions of a priest in the early nine-teenth century.

As this book amounts to the only theological course that Abbé Vianney followed it will repay a little examination. Its full title reads *Instructions sur le rituel contenant la théorie et la pratique des sacrements et de la morale et tous les principes et décisions necéssaires au ministère écclésiastique*. The edition used by Abbé Vianney was published in 1780, but the book appeared originally some thirty years earlier. It was written by Louis-Albert-Joly de Choin, Bishop of Toulon from 1738 until his death in 1759, who revived we are told, "the simplicity of the early days of the Church, kept his revenues to distribute them to the poor, and would employ no vicar-general in the administration of his diocese since he wished that all business should pass through his own hands". From the preface we learn that the book was never intended as a theological course, and the fact is clear enough from the title. It was meant as a book of instruction for priests in the administration of their parish and dealt with all matters that a competent and zealous pastor should know. By far the greater part is concerned with the sacrament of penance, but all the sacraments are mentioned, and other matters as well, some of them in considerable detail. There is a long section, for instance, on the duties of canons, how they are to behave themselves in choir, how much money they are entitled to out of the revenues if they miss a part of the daily office, and the system to be observed in the distribution of the capitular revenues. There is a chapter on preaching, on the fees to which a clergyman is entitled, and the complicated subject of Mass stipends. Parish priests are told that if a child is brought for baptism, if a woman comes to be churched, "with much clamour and the sound of musical instruments", they are to postpone the ceremony.

On the sacraments there is a short dogmatic summary, but principally the treatment is practical and concerned with the details of canon law and rubrics and those parts of moral theology that are relevant in this connexion. On the subject of penance the bishop is very lengthy. Here, on the ten commandments and the commandments of the Church, he writes what amounts to a small treatise of moral theology in an elegant eighteenth-century French with much quotation from the Fathers and the early Councils.

There is a good deal more in the book than this. Abbé Vianney will have learned from it how to say the breviary and all the casuistry concerning it. He will have derived from it some notion of what a devoted parish priest should be, and have discovered that his housekeeper must be over forty, and, if possible, ugly. He will have found that as an ecclesiastic he must not frequent inns (save on a journey, and then only so far as necessary), that the theatre was forbidden to him under pain of suspension, that he could not bear arms or go hunting. Abbé Balley probably told him that these prescriptions also formed part of the synodal statutes of the diocese of Lyon.

There is no doubt that Mgr Joly de Choin was a rigorist and that his book was written for times very different from those immediate post-revolutionary years when Abbé Vianney was poring over it in the study at Ecully. Yet it probably reflected closely enough Abbé Balley's views—he had been trained under the *ancien régime*—and the manual in use at the seminary at Lyon, in its section on moral theology, was equally severe. On the proper conduct of public worship Mgr de Choin laid great emphasis: he castigates priests who were slovenly in their manner of saying Mass, and considers half an hour a reasonable time for a low Mass. Here Abbé Vianney had a fine example before him in the person of his tutor, who, we are told, said Mass always with great devotion that moved those who were present; in this Abbé Vianney copied him.

On a final analysis, therefore, it cannot be said that Abbé Vianney learned much theology; from his manual he obtained a little moral theology and a little canon law, almost no dogma, no Scripture, and only a few practical notions of liturgy. Thus equipped, after three months' study, he was presented by his tutor at the examination held at the seminary for the approaching ordination. Once more he had to face the board of examiners, with M. Bochard, one of the vicars-general, as chairman. Once

more his nerve failed him, he hardly understood the Latin questions and was only able to mumble a word or two of not very
good sense in reply. But this time the examiners were in a somewhat delicate position. It was known that this candidate had been
specially tutored by Abbé Balley, a well-known and venerated
priest of the diocese, that he was, so to say, sponsoring the candidate. "It is unlike M. Balley to send us an unsuitable candidate,"
we can hear them muttering, "yet it is obviously impossible to
let him through." In the end they resolved the difficulty by saying
that they could not under the regulations admit Abbé Vianney to
orders, but that of course he was free to try another diocese if he
could find a bishop.

On learning the news M. Balley was upset. What is more, he
was growing a little tired of the diocesan authorities and the
continual obstacles that they gave him to surmount. He blamed
them for the muddle about Abbé Vianney's call-up, for sending
him away from the seminary, and now for this last difficulty. It
must be put right. The very next morning he was in Lyon
assembling his forces. The first call was on M. Groboz, now
secretary of the diocese, his fellow-missioner during the Terror,
the priest who gave Vianney his first communion.

"You remember young Vianney from Dardilly?" he inquired.
"You heard his first confession and gave him his first communion."
Abbé Groboz remembered young Vianney perfectly.

Abbé Balley told him all the circumstances, laying particular
emphasis on his piety and the certainty of his vocation; all that
stood in the way, he concluded, was the little matter of knowledge
of the Latin language. Abbé Groboz promised to use his influence. On, then, to M. Bochard, where the two priests insisted
afresh. M. Bochard promised to study the matter. But Abbé
Balley wanted more than this. He invited the vicar-general to
come to Ecully and question the young man in French. "Bring
the superior of the seminary with you," was his parting shot.

Next day in the study at Ecully, in familiar surroundings, with
the presence of his tutor to reassure him and the benefit of questions put in a language that he could understand, Abbé Vianney
made a good impression on his examiners. M. Bochard and his

companion left Ecully to report to the principal vicar-general, M. Courbon, in charge of the diocese during the absence of Cardinal Fesch, then in exile in Rome.

M. Courbon listened to what he was told, inquired if the young man was devout, and on hearing that he was, decided to admit him to the subdiaconate. He was moved probably by the example of Cardinal Fesch, who a couple of years earlier, without examination, had ordained subdeacon all the seminarists over twenty-one who presented themselves for ordination. Those who did not come forward were sent away from the seminary, thus becoming liable to be called up into the army. Cardinal Fesch was afraid that a military reverse would empty his seminary since he was assured that all those not in orders would be taken for the army. As Napoleon was then in Russia the Cardinal's fear was not without grounds. In addition, M. Courbon was certainly influenced by the fact that the candidate was vouched for by Abbé Balley, who was held in high esteem in the diocese.

On July 2, therefore, in the primatial church of Lyon, from the hands of Mgr Simon, Bishop of Grenoble, Abbé Vianney received the four minor orders and the subdiaconate. He had prepared for them by a month's retreat at the seminary and had there been instructed on the powers that he was about to receive. Back again at Ecully under Abbé Balley's charge he began on his final preparation for the priesthood.

The twelve months from July 1814 to June 1815 saw events of some consequence in France; in 1814 Napoleon went into exile on Elba and on April 14 of that year Louis XVIII had been proclaimed King of France and Navarre. In March 1815 Napoleon set foot on French soil once more, his brief appearance culminating in the defeat at Waterloo. Abbé Balley and his pupil no doubt had news of these events at Ecully but they were not caught up in them. The seminarists in Lyon, on the other hand, and the chapter of St Jean were royalists to a man, and when Cardinal Fesch ventured to return to his diocese, for three days only, on his way to Paris, where his nephew called for his presence in this crisis of his affairs, he received an equivocal reception. He had heard that the seminarists refused to sing *Domine salvum fac imperatorem*

4

nostrum Napoleonem after Mass, and fearing that their conduct would cause the closing of the establishment, went to remonstrate with them. The young men kept to their rooms, and it was with difficulty that a few were gathered together by one of the vicars-general to hear the Cardinal's remarks. As he left the seminary one of the young men chalked *Vive le Roi* on his carriage, and with this seditious sentiment displayed he set out for Paris, passing from his diocese, and this story, never to return.

Meanwhile at Ecully the *Rituel de Toulon* was once more laid under contribution. Work went on for nine months, and at the end of May Abbé Vianney was back at the seminary for his immediate preparation for the diaconate. He received this order on the eve of the festival of St John the Baptist from the hands of Mgr Simon in company with his friend Marcellin Champagnat and Jean-Claude Colin, the founder of the Society of Mary, or Marist Fathers. Immediately after this, Abbé Balley was busy once more, and as a result of his negotiations M. Bochard travelled down to Ecully at the beginning of July and examined Abbé Vianney with a view to his ordination to the priesthood. "The learned examiner questioned Abbé Vianney for more than hour on the most difficult questions of moral theology," writes Mgr Trochu. "He was pleased with his answers, and even astonished at his clearness and accuracy." One can only suppose this to be one of these slight exaggerations to which the hagiographical style lends itself. Abbé Bochard was surprised, more probably, that the young man could resolve the ordinary cases put before him, so displaying more common sense than he had credited him with. He was well aware of the gaps in his knowledge. However, he passed him as fit to be presented to M. Courbon, who gave him his dimissorial letters to the Bishop of Grenoble. Faculties for hearing confessions could wait until he had been a priest for a little while. The vicar-general's remark, as he signed the letters, seems to reveal something of what Abbé Bochard had reported to him. "It is not only learned priests that the Church needs," he said, "but, still more, devoted priests."

CHAPTER IV

ABBÉ BALLEY'S NEW CURATE

THE sixty-five miles that separate Lyon from Grenoble may nowadays be travelled by train or over the road which runs straight to Bourgoin, where it branches right for Chambéry and Savoy and left for Grenoble and the south. It is not one of the most interesting of French roads, though at the beginning of the nineteenth century it passed through unspoiled countryside, and even now its monotony is relieved by the view of the mountains behind Grenoble. Abbé Vianney undertook the journey from Ecully to Grenoble on foot. On 9 August 1815, in Lyon, he received his dimissorial letters from M. Courbon; on the evening of 12 August, a Saturday, he was in Grenoble. He walked, then, at least sixteen miles a day, and probably more, for we do not know the time of his arrival. The journey was certainly accomplished with greater alacrity than that upon which a few years previously he had set out on his way from Roanne to rejoin his unit. Then he had managed but eight miles or so before he turned aside, now there was no turning aside; he pressed on eagerly.

Under the scorching August sun his cassock was hot, but it is unlikely that he wore over it the long black coat affected out of doors by the clergymen of Paris, and encouraged for use in the diocese of Lyon by the Cardinal Archbishop. His scanty baggage contained an alb for his ordination, a little food and a breviary. And the journey was not without its hazards. The roads were infested with Austrian troops; he was suspected of being a spy, was threatened more than once, but came through safely, the simplicity of his answers turning away the wrath of the invaders.

He had much to think about as he trudged along. There were the resolutions of his ordination retreat to be kept fresh in mind, and he could not help looking back on all his struggles towards the goal that he was now rapidly approaching, nor forbear a prayer for his mother, whose help he remembered with gratitude. M. Balley, back in Ecully, was, he knew, praying for him; for this other principal supporter of him in all his trials he had immense affection. He thought of this man who, though not yet seventy, had been rendered infirm by his austerities and rough life under the Terror, saying Mass in the little church at Ecully, slowly and reverently, some times overcome by weeping, going about his parish every soul of which was known to him, always encouraging and helpful, a father rather than a stern taskmaster to the village people. He had resolved to imitate him so far as he could. He visualized him saying his breviary in church, always on his knees without support, regularly in the same place four times a day, always up early in the morning, leading a penitential life, eating little but always hospitable, never wasting a moment, so that when he was not out in his parish or in church he was at his books in the study. Abbé Vianney felt that in Abbé Balley he had a model that would be hard to equal among the clergy of France.

For a year now Abbé Vianney had said the breviary; he was punctual in reciting it as he journeyed towards Grenoble. He was fond of praying in the open air, and though his Latin was too sketchy for him to make out the meaning of the lessons at Matins, particularly when they were from St Ambrose, the psalms by constant use were beginning to become familiar to him, and Abbé Balley had to some extent explained them. The hymns were difficult, but those recurring daily at the Little Hours, once painfully translated, could be remembered.

It was the liturgy of Lyon that he used all his life, a medieval variant of the Roman rite that, escaping St Pius V's changes in 1568, fell a prey to the reforming itch of the eighteenth-century bishops. Abbé Vianney used the edition of the breviary published in 1815 under the authority of Cardinal Fesch, and a copy of this edition is to be found among the relics preserved at Ars, though it is probable that he did not acquire it until a year or two later, and before and during the early years of his priesthood said his office from an older book, obtained possibly from Abbé Balley.

Before it underwent the process known as reform the liturgy of Lyon was performed in all its splendour in the primatial church of St John. One of the most striking features of the history of the chapter there was the subordinate position occupied by the arch-bishop in his own cathedral. The canons, with their quaint head-dress resembling a mitre, ruled there with vigour. Irregular it may have been, but the conservatism of the chapter managed to preserve their ancient liturgical heritage until the latter half of the eighteenth century—much later than many other dioceses in France—and it was only after the archbishop had managed to impose his rule in his own cathedral that one of them, de Montazet, even then with difficulty succeeded in securing the adoption by the canons of a breviary and missal fashioned after the latest Paris recension.

According to the rules of the chapter, he who was to sing Mass next morning must be present at Vespers and Matins, and no exception was made for the archbishop. As late as 1734, on the occasion of the jubilee at the cathedral, on St John the Baptist's day, the archbishop and his suite went to a firework display and on this account were unable to be back in time for Matins. Neither he nor his suite was admitted to the chapter Mass, or to Vespers the following evening.

The canons said the office by heart, using a book only at the lectern for the lessons at Matins and a small one for the officiant to sing the little chapters and collects. Hymns at Lyon were a late introduction, and so, I imagine, were farsings. Towards the end of the seventeenth century they used to farse the *Benedicamus Domino* on feast days: thus at Christmas Lauds the choirboys sang *Benedicamus Domino, noé, noé, noé, voici le temps où Dieu est né*, a chant that the archbishop contrived to have abolished because, he remarked, the choirboys mispronounced it and it was unworthy of the Church of Lyon. "One would think," he added, "they were calling on old father Noah who planted the vine!"

The Paris breviary on which the reformed breviary of Lyon was modelled was shorter than the Roman of those days; in general its length corresponded to that of the Roman since the reform of Pius X. The Psalter reminds one very much of the distribution adopted by Pius X, but it is not identical and some of the psalms are more split up. Not only in Easter week, but all through Eastertide,

Matins has only one nocturn of three psalms and three lessons. One of the principal features of these French breviaries was the exclusion so far as possible of "ecclesiastical compositions", and so the lovely Christmas anthems and the rest disappear in favour of neatly chosen Scripture texts, all appropriate to the feast but without the joyous solemnity of the Roman anthems.

The hymns are for the most part those which were written or rewritten by Santueil and Coffin.[1] The text of such offices as that of St Peter's Chair (there is one feast only on January 18, entitled *Pontificatus seu Cathedrae S. Petri qua primum Antiochae sedit tum Romae*) betrays their origin. The sentiments expressed are all admirable, but significantly the invitatory is no longer *Tu es pastor ovium, princeps Apostolorum*, and one misses many of the beautiful responsories and anthems of the Gregorian responsorial. True, all was taken from Scripture, but the compilers of these French breviaries seemed to try to make of the office a vehicle of instruction and edification rather than of praise and prayer. These breviaries, that of Lyon among them, reflected the religious spirit of the eighteenth century and display an almost unbearable pedantry and a literary self-consciousness that is at times well-nigh unbelievable.

This digression about the liturgy of Lyon as it was used by Abbé Vianney all his life has been given because liturgy forms an essential element in the existence of any priest and is the background to his days. It reflects, too, something of the religious atmosphere in which Abbé Vianney was brought up and lived. Lyon and the surrounding countryside has always evinced a

---

[1] For the benefit of readers interested in Latin hymnography I give the text of the hymn at None recited all his priestly life by Abbé Vianney; it has not the austere beauty of *Rerum Deus tenax vigor*, but it does show a certain inspiration tha is lacking in many eighteenth-century hymns:

> *Prono volutus impetu,*
> *Inclinat in noctem dies,*
> *Sic vita supremam cito*
> *Festinat ad metam gradu.*
> *O Christe, dum fixus cruci*
> *Expandis orbi brachia,*
> *Amare da crucem, tuo*
> *Da nos in amplexu mori.*
>
> *Deo Patri, etc.*

sturdy independence of thought, and the phrase *nous autres Lyonnais*, frequently on the lips of the inhabitants of those parts, is a characteristic expression of this state of mind.

Some time on the Saturday, 12 August, Abbé Vianney made his way through the streets of Grenoble to the seminary. There, in what before the Revolution had been the chapel belonging to the Minims, Jean-Marie-Baptiste Vianney was ordained priest on the thirteenth Sunday after Pentecost by Mgr Simon, the local bishop. He said his first Mass in the seminary chapel the next morning, 14 August, the vigil of the Assumption, remained in the seminary for the feast next day and started back on his way to Ecully on 16 August, once more travelling on foot.

With this achievement of all that he had hoped for and looked forward to for a long time past emerges a characteristic of what his life was to be very largely for the rest of his years, for he began to experience the loneliness that is the common lot of the priest in his daily life, particularly the parish priest of a small country village; at his ordination and first Mass he had a foretaste of it for not one relation or friend was there with him. The bishop ordained him by himself in the seminary chapel during vacation time; at next day's Mass he was just one of those celebrating in the chapel, two chaplains of the Austrian army saying Mass at neighbouring altars. He trudged back the sixty-five miles to Lyon and on to Ecully alone and it was only on arrival there that he could share his joy with Abbé Balley and Madame Bibost, his friends.

At Ecully he found work to do in plenty. Abbé Balley was zealous and hard-working, but he was getting old and was glad to obtain his former pupil's services as curate. M. Courbon had confirmed the appointment. Abbé Vianney set to with a will, all the pent-up energy and enthusiasm of the past years of frustration now finding an outlet in that work which he had desired so ardently since his days as a hand on his father's farm.

He visited the sick, he preached, he catechized and baptized. He could not yet hear confessions. M. Balley reminded him that he must not neglect the *Rituel de Toulon*, which still required to be studied in view of the faculties that must be applied for before very long. Preaching cost him a considerable effort. He spent hours on his preparation: "in the pulpit he was short but clear" we are told, though his sister Gothon, who walked over from Dardilly to hear him, did not consider that he preached well. The matter of his sermons was simple enough, and on one topic he found matter enough in Mgr de Choin's invaluable manual. Dancing was much in vogue in Ecully; the new curate castigated it in no uncertain terms.

The two priests lived together, vying with each other in mortification, particularly in the matter of food. A few potatoes, a crust of bread, a little water sufficed them; a joint of boiled beef which the housekeeper carried in day after day, beginning to show signs of its great age, had to be thrown away. But visiting priests were always hospitably entertained. The statutes of the diocese of Lyon call for common life among the clergy of a parish: Abbé Balley and his curate observed this to the full, even performing their devotions together, going on a pilgrimage to Our Lady of Fourvière; a strange-looking couple no doubt as, sheltering under the same umbrella, they made their way up the hillside from the Place Bellecour to the church that dominates Lyon. At least when they arrived there they were spared the sight of the hideous basilica put up by Pierre Bossan at the end of last century.

After some months Abbé Balley obtained faculties for his curate and was himself the first penitent of this man whose especial work was to be the confessional. Once it became known that the new curate could now absolve them the parishioners began to flock to him and on certain days he was kept busy. A year and a half went by, filled with prayer, a certain amount of study, and work for the people of Ecully, who began to hold him in affection. In February an ulcer on the leg confined Abbé Balley to his bed, which he hardly left again. Practically speaking Abbé Vianney ran the parish as the parish priest's health grew worse; gangrene set in towards the end of the year and he died on December 17, having received the last sacraments from the man, who, humanly speaking, owed him the fulfilment of his vocation. By the death of Abbé Balley, Abbé Vianney lost a father, a counsellor and above all a friend. He was to mourn him for the rest of his days. Right up to the end of his life he was heard to declare, "If I were a painter I could still do a portrait of him." He regarded him as a saint: "I have encountered some beautiful souls in my time," he remarked on one occasion, "but none so fine as his." And to the end of his life he kept by him, over the fireplace in his presbytery, the little mirror that belonged to his friend; he did so because it had reflected that much-loved face.

A few parishioners desired to keep Abbé Vianney as parish priest, but they failed to convince him that he should apply for the post, and it was unlikely, in any event, that a relatively untried curate should be given this responsible post. He served for some weeks under the new parish priest, Abbé Tripier, but he was not Abbé Balley, and Abbé Vianney found it difficult to accommodate himself to new ways at the presbytery. In February he was appointed to Ars, a little village in the department of Ain, some eighteen miles to the north of Ecully.

* * *

We have come to an end of a chapter in Abbé Vianney's life. All that precedes in this story of thirty-two years and leads up to his appointment as parish priest of an obscure village tucked away in the countryside north of Lyon forms the preparation for his life-work, all of which was carried out in that village and the neighbouring district. We have seen him journeying from his native Dardilly to Noës, to Louvesc, to Grenoble. He never went further afield than that; he never saw the sea; he never visited Paris; practically speaking, he never left that corner of France in which he was born, brought up, and trained for the priesthood. If ever there was a prophet who remained in his own country it was Abbé Vianney.

In the course of the narrative it has emerged to some extent what manner of man he was. It is clear that at this point of his life he already gave ample promise of being a devoted parish priest, a man who would care for his flock and work himself to death to save their souls and, by leading them to heaven, arrive there himself. He was generous by nature, giving not only his goods to the poor but giving himself unsparingly. He was not easily diverted from doing what he saw was clearly his duty, though in the past he had given way to discouragement and needed Abbé Balley's firm conviction to restore his confidence. He was pleasant to meet, and attracted people, he had a sense of humour, though so far it has not come out very clearly, he was strong and he was greatly given to mortification. He possessed that peasant common-sense and sharpness which is a standby in any emergency, and by upbringing and ancestry he understood country people. As he set off for his new parish he went there with the determination, for the good of the souls committed to him, to make it the best parish in the diocese, not for his own vainglory, with no thought of counting heads or financial success, but solely for the glory of God. In becoming a priest, in rising from being a farmhand to being a Curé, he had no idea of bettering himself; he never considered himself as being above his people, he regarded himself as one of them, and so indeed he was and remained.

PART II

(1818-1827)

CHAPTER V

ABBÉ VIANNEY'S FIRST PARISH

ON 9 February 1818, as night was falling, Abbé Vianney, accompanied by *Mère* Bibost and followed at a little distance by an ox-cart led by one of his friends from Ecully, was within a mile or two of his new parish. The cart carried his few bits of furniture, Abbé Balley's bed and books that had been bequeathed to him, and *Mère* Bibost's scanty possessions. They had journeyed thus on foot from Ecully to Trévoux, and there, leaving the main road, branched off to the right towards Ars, some five miles away. Abbé Vianney was on his way to his own parish; it was a solemn moment in his life, but it has to be confessed that he had been given the least important parish in the diocese of Lyon. This corner of it, formerly belonging to the diocese of Belley, and comprising the civil *département* of Ain, for ten or fifteen years had been generally regarded as the region to which difficult or wayward priests were sent to cool their heels. In Abbé Vianney's case there was no question of this, but someone was required at Ars, and M. Courbon sent him with the thought, probably, that it was not a parish to which he need assign one of his better-endowed priests: no learning would be required to look after the peasants at Ars, and if the earnest young Abbé Vianney could effect a change for the better he would not be left there off the map for always. As events turned out Abbé Vianney put Ars very much on the map and remained there for the rest of his days.

From Ecully the small party had followed the course of the Saône, traversing the pleasantly wooded countryside with its richly fertile soil bordered by the river as it flowed to Lyon, where its slow clear waters mingle with the swift-moving slaty Rhône. Trévoux dominates the valley of the Saône, but there the party left the river behind them and made off to the right over the gently undulating country. As travellers by night can set their course by the stars, so Abbé Vianney on that February afternoon found his way by the church spires. Between Trévoux and Ars, at one time or another St Didier, Ste Euphémie to the left, Toussieux far away to the right, Misérieux straight in front, gave him an idea of where he was. It grows dark early in February; already the tower of Misérieux had disappeared behind them in the mist and darkness of the evening, when, after inquiry, the party found the road leading down into Ars. They walked down the village street with its straggling cottages from which already lights were showing in the gloom, discerned the church standing on the left and next door to it the presbytery, a modest peasant-type dwelling of five rooms: dining-room and kitchen on the ground floor with three bedrooms above.

The ringing of the church bell for Mass next morning informed the inhabitants that they had a new parish priest. The first few days were spent getting to know his way about, in examining his church and probably in setting it to rights as far as he could. The church of Ars, for all that it went back to the twelfth century, gave no appearance of beauty or dignity. It was a very ordinary-looking, almost ugly, yellowish building with plain windows and surmounted by a primitive erection, of four wooden planks, with a cross-beam to carry the cracked bell, this somewhat odd construction replacing the tower which had fallen down some years beforehand.

One of Abbé Vianney's tasks during the first few days was to call on the local château and there persuade the lady of the manor, Mlle des Garets, to take back from the presbytery some of the furniture that she had lent for the comfort of the priest. He had no use, he told her, for the many cooking utensils, the large roasting dish and spit, the armchairs, the six dining-room chairs, the two beds with testers and so on; he would keep for his use an ordinary bed for visitors, two old tables, a bookshelf, cupboards, straw-bottomed chairs, a cast-iron cooking pot and one or two other articles. For his own bed he already possessed that bequeathed to him by Abbé Balley.

On Sunday 13 February, the new parish priest was installed. He was not properly speaking the parish priest since Ars was a chapel-of-ease to Misérieux and it was the parish priest of that

place who came to perform the ceremony, but in popular estima-
tion Abbé Vianney was henceforward known as Curé d'Ars and
some years later the parish of Ars was canonically established.

Abbé Vianney at once set about the conversion of his parish.
That may seem perhaps a strong term to use; it is justified nevertheless. A period without a priest, a time when one priest had to
serve five parishes, followed by the short pastorate of a young man
who came to Ars only to die of consumption at the age of twenty-
seven, and all this preceded by the days of the Revolution when,
the church closed, the parish priest apostatized and set up in business in the village in which he had ministered, were all circumstances which brought religion to a low ebb. The people were not
instructed and the influence of the Church had dwindled to an
extent that the peasants had reverted to a way of life in which
Christianity seemed to play little part. Few came to church and
fewer still went to the sacraments. The hard work of the fields,
combined with the relaxing atmosphere of the valley in which
Ars was set, seemed to leave them neither energy nor leisure to
rise above the material things that formed the ingredients of their
daily struggle for a frugal living. Their recreation they took in
dancing, in drinking in the taverns, of which there were four to
serve the sixty houses of the village, and in the long winter's night
social gatherings held in some barn. Churchgoing as a habit had
been lost and other things, proved by experience to be more
exciting, had taken its place.

Abbé Vianney's first concern was to make contact with his
people. He visited all the houses in the parish, going out every day
at noon when he knew that the people would be home for the
midday meal. Dressed in his cassock, which was already beginning to turn green with age, and on his feet his heavy peasant
boots, patched and many times re-soled, his large clerical hat
under his arm (he was never known to wear it), he would appear
as a family were at table. Sometimes he was offered a meal, but
always refused on the excuse that he had already dined, though
his dinner had consisted probably of a crust of bread and a potato
or two. *Mère* Bibost did not stay long when she saw that the
cooking that she was required to do amounted to nothing more

than boiling a few potatoes from time to time. He would chat about the things that were familiar to all of them: the work of the fields, the crops, the price of wool at the market at Anse or Neuville, the quality of last year's Beaujolais maturing in the cellars of these small homesteads.

He managed nevertheless to find out about each family, the number of children, the state of their religious instruction, the difficulties that each had to face. He discovered, too, that there were still some good families in the parish; the Renards with a son at the seminary at Lyon, the Mandys (Antoine Mandy was mayor), the Lassagnes whose daughter Catherine was to become his devoted helper, Michel Cimier and Jean Verchère.

He came to the conclusion that ignorance rather than malice was his chief enemy in the work he was endeavouring to do. Many of his parishioners (those particularly who had grown up during the Revolution) had no knowledge of even the elements of the catechism. These formed the hard core of resistance, and as they had never known anything better than their present way of life they were sometimes inclined to boast about it.

The daily routine of the new parish priest's life began to take shape and as he investigated the flock committed to his care his parishioners observed the pattern of his days. In a small community like the village of Ars it is very difficult to live a life that is hidden from the eyes of one's neighbours. It soon became known, therefore, that the Curé's lantern could be observed long before dawn as he picked his way over the flagstones from the presbytery to the side door of the church and that he spent the time praying there until he said Mass. It was common knowledge too that in the morning if he were needed it was useless to knock at the presbytery door, he would always be found in church. Gradually news went round the village about the new Curé's simple methods of housekeeping; people told each other how he cooked a saucepan of potatoes and when they were done hung them up in a wire basket on the wall whence he would take a couple at midday, and how at the end of the week, though those remaining were covered with mildew, he made no bones about eating them. Tales were told of the sound of his discipline that could be heard

THE ROAD FROM ROANNE TO NOËS

ABBÉ VIANNEY'S PULPIT

at night, and the woman, *Mère* Renard, who sometimes went to tidy up the presbytery, revealed that bloodstains were to be found in the bedroom.

His life was hard and penitential, yet he inflicted on himself further severe corporal mortifications: the discipline at night, lack of sleep, instruments of penance, the hairshirt inherited from Abbé Balley, all formed part of his campaign for the conversion of his parish. After his perfunctory midday meal he set out to visit his flock and on occasion enjoyed a walk in the woods or over the fields. He would take his breviary and wander along, praying as he went, his whole being absorbed, and oblivious of his surroundings or of an occasional observer, falling to his knees or bowing profoundly. So he was seen once kneeling in the woods, the tears running down his face, exclaiming aloud, "My God, convert my parish!"

On one occasion *Mère* Bibost and his sister Gothon journeyed from Dardilly to visit him. There was hardly anything to eat in the house and Abbé Vianney was constrained to offer them some of the mouldy potatoes from the basket on the wall. They had, however, taken the precaution of buying some bread *en route* and discovered eggs and flour that had been given to the parish priest by one of his flock (and promptly forgotten by him). With these ingredients they set about cooking *matefaims*, a local delicacy mentioned by Brillat-Savarin. It is a kind of griddle cake, easily made, and often used by the peasants as a substitute for bread. And they killed two pigeons and roasted them. When Abbé Vianney came in from church and was confronted with this meal his chief concern was for the pigeons. He acknowledged that he was worried about these birds because he was afraid that they damaged the neighbours' crops, but he had never meant to kill them. He refused to touch anything save one of the *matefaims*.

When his elder brother came to see him there was nothing at all in the house and François was obliged to dig potatoes and cook them. *Mère* Renard, who in succession to *Mère* Bibost held the very honorary position of cook, soon lost courage. She would prepare a dish of *matefaims* and take them to the presbytery, only to find them untouched and mouldering on the table a few days later. Abbé Vianney has left an account of how he sometimes cooked *matefaims* for himself; his consisted of flour and water only, and he would eat the first while the second was cooking, and the second while the third was cooking, and the third as he tidied up the grate. If Brillat-Savarin had been called on to sample them he would not have felt inclined to praise this local delicacy. Sometimes his parishioners gave him a loaf of good white bread, but as quickly he gave it away again to beggars, offering them a *sou* for the crust or buying from them the old crusts that they carried in the bottom of their sacks.

For nine years, until 1827, Abbé Vianney lived in this fashion; his diet was only modified when the orphanage was founded and he began to take a little food there. In his penances he certainly crossed the bounds of prudence and, in after-years, speaking of these early days of his ministry, he referred to his "youthful madness" and remarked, "When a man's young he acts rashly".

To prayer and penance he added the eloquence at his command to instruct his parishioners in church. His first sermons cost him an immense effort. He prepared them with care. With the aid of a collection of the lives of the saints, the Catechism of the Council of Trent, Rodriguez's *Christian Perfection*, Bergier's theological dictionary, and someone's book of sermons, he wrote out his discourses at length. He had never been much good at his books, and the effort at actual composition, for he wrote out every word, took him some time. Occasionally he would leave the sacristy, where he wrote on the vestment press, and go to kneel before the altar. He spent hours in this way with his preparation. Once it was all down on paper he set about learning it by heart, thirty or forty pages of it covered with his straggling writing, with never a paragraph and hardly a margin. His memory had always been poor. When he thought that he had mastered his sermon he would try it out in the churchyard late on Saturday night and passers-by sometimes caught him at it.

The congregation for which these sermons were prepared was scanty enough. A few old peasant women, the lady of the manor, perhaps a couple of men and some of the children. And the new parish priest made so much noise at it that they could not go to

sleep. He shouted. After the Gospel at the sung Mass on Sunday
morning, when he put off his chasuble and went up the rickety
wooden steps to the pulpit, they knew that he would be there for a
good hour, that they would be forced to listen and that they
would hear nothing for their comfort.

Examples of these sermons of his early days at Ars are still
extant. In later years, when he ceased to write them down beforehand and preached, not without preparation but without the set
form that he at first adopted, the whole style was changed. In
those first months as a parish priest he preached to his flock about
the proper way to behave in church, about keeping Sundays holy
and the purpose of his work in Ars as their parish priest, which
was, he told them, to lead them all to heaven. His instructions
were moral rather than dogmatic; dancing and frequentation of
taverns earned his severest reproof.

There were occasions when Abbé Vianney lost the thread of his
sermon, stumbled over a phrase and, remembering no more, was
obliged to leave the pulpit. It was hardly surprising that it should
be so. After a short night, worn out with his efforts to learn it all
by heart, undernourished, and still fasting at perhaps nearly eleven
of a Sunday morning, he could hardly have expected it to be
otherwise. There came a time when, caught in the pulpit and
remembering nothing of his carefully written sermon, he began to
improvise and in doing so found himself as a preacher. What
he said came from his heart and tumbled eloquently from his lips.
And thus his whole style was changed and from being artificial
became natural and consequently more effective. He had something to say and he said it simply, thus involuntarily following the
golden rule of public speaking. Improvisation in the pulpit, as on
the platform, to be effective requires preparation; Abbé Vianney's
preparation is to be found in his long periods of prayer every
morning in his church, in his penances and fasting and in his conviction of the immense task that he must accomplish in his parish.

Easter 1818 had proved a heavy blow to him; many of his
parishioners, among the men particularly, did not come to confession and communion. Some of them had not been to the sacraments for fifteen or twenty years. He saw clearly that the work

facing him was going to be a long and uphill struggle. He was filled with a sense of his own insufficiency, but he did not lose courage. He had made up his mind that he would lead them to heaven, and to heaven they should go. He saw clearly, too, the steps that he would have to take. Young and old must be instructed; they must know their faith. Sunday work must cease. As summer drew on and the harvest approached, even the children passed their Sundays in the fields. The feasts of the Church must be kept religiously, and for this to be done the dancing which took place, even in the open air just outside the parish church, must be stopped. The four taverns in Ars, which had formed the subject of more than one sermon, must be closed and so remove temptation from the men who frequented them instead of coming to Mass.

That was the programme. He set about it resolutely.

CHAPTER VI

THE CONVERSION OF ARS

ON assigning Abbé Vianney to Ars, M. Courbon said to him, "There is no great love of God in this parish; it will be your job to make it grow there". In setting about the conversion of Ars, Abbé Vianney with his four-point programme of the work to be done was endeavouring to carry out the vicar-general's instructions, though at the beginning it rather looked as if he was imbuing his parishioners with the fear of hell rather than with the love of God.

During his first weeks in the parish curiosity to observe the new priest and the absence of urgent work in the fields resulted in a fair sprinkling of people in the nave of a Sunday morning; with the coming of spring the congregation was reduced to a handful. Early in the morning the peasants were off to the fields, only returning as the light failed, to put on their best clothes and go dancing, or drinking in the taverns.

About all these things Abbé Vianney adopted an attitude that seems to us nowadays extremely severe, and in his first years as a parish priest a rigorist he certainly was. In this he was not alone for he was of his times and it would have been difficult for him to have been anything else. An examination of the manuals of moral theology current at the period and their attitude to dancing or the theatre, for instance, shows this conclusively. In addition, the notions that he had imbibed from the *Rituel de Toulon*, combined with the special circumstances of his parish, inclined him to adopt an attitude that we find unduly harsh regarding what of their nature are legitimate pleasures and recreation. His mentor, Mgr Joly de Choin, the author of the *Rituel de Toulon*, certainly went too far, we should say nowadays, in forbidding categorically the theatre and all dancing. Abbé Vianney shared the bishop's views on theatricals, though at Ars the theatre was not one of the besetting temptations of the parishioners. Both master and pupil were in line with an attitude that among Christians goes back to the days of the primitive Church and, in Abbé Vianney's day, was commonly to be encountered among churchmen. So far as the theatre is concerned this attitude was not shared by one priest, who was born in 1815, three days after Abbé Vianney's ordination; in 1847, Don Bosco, not so very far away in north Italy, was encouraging his boys to act and was writing plays for them; among the eyebrows raised were those of Mgr Dupanloup, who knew and on occasion consulted both men.

Taking down from the shelf holding Abbé Balley's bequest of books the much thumbed *Rituel de Toulon*, Abbé Vianney read that Mgr Joly de Choin regarded the theatre as a proximate occasion of mortal sin and that those who frequent the theatre and those who act on the stage or entertain in other ways (strolling players, jugglers, conjurors and the like: the sort who appear at village fairs for instance) are to be refused absolution if they will not give it up; actors who die while exercising their profession are to be refused Christian burial.

Possibly Abbé Vianney did not trouble to re-read what the bishop said about the theatre, but he certainly learned every word that was said about dancing and followed the instructions to the letter.

"Dancing", he read, "is not of its nature sinful or wrong; but as very rarely it does not become sinful, by reason of the different circumstances almost always attending it, it is wise for a Christian to abstain from it. This is what St Charles Borromeo says concerning dances: 'Sad and frequent experience must make us recognize that in this exceedingly corrupt world gatherings for dances or balls, ballets and others things of this nature, are the unfortunate source of several sins, and even of the greatest and most grievous, because the filthiest thoughts, accompanied by actions and words equally sinful, are their almost inevitable consequence; at them Christian morals are corrupted because almost always they result in a pernicious and fatal proclivity for the pleasures of the flesh and all kinds of sensuality'.

"And indeed it is not possible to justify or to regard as innocent gatherings of this sort which, we see, are condemned by the Holy Spirit. 'Use not much the company of her that is a dancer, and hearken not to her, lest thou perish by the force of her charms' (*Ecclesiasticus* 9. 4). Of dances St Ambrose says, *delicarium comes atque luxuriae saltatio* . . .

"There is no cause for astonishment that the holy Fathers should have spoken so strongly against this kind of amusement which the circumstances of time, the persons of different sexes present, the songs and the like, render almost always sinful. These gatherings are arranged, held and frequented only for the pleasure of the senses. They are composed of entirely worldly people, filled with the spirit of the world, the company and the very sight of whom can only be very harmful. Men and women there foregather with all that makes for pleasure, that is calculated to inspire passion in each other; the familiarity allowed (at such gatherings) cannot fail to make an impression on the heart, the gestures that are made, the pose adopted by those that dance, who seek solely to please, can only kindle the fire of concupiscence; the music, the harmony of the instruments, the tunes that are played, weaken the heart and render it susceptible to the most vivid and tender impressions and it is not possible to obey the command of the Holy Spirit: 'Gaze not upon a maiden, lest her beauty be a stumbling block to thee. Turn away thy face from a woman dressed up, and gaze not about upon another's beauty. For many have perished by the beauty of a woman, and hereby lust is enkindled as a fire' (*Ecclesiasticus* 9. 5, 8, 9) . . . It is true that St Thomas regarded dancing in itself as innocent and free from sin if those who dance can do so with decency and without giving scandal; if propriety is regularly observed in regard to songs, gestures, the place, the time and other attendant circumstances, if all that is not fitting for a Christian is banished from these gatherings; but this holy doctor adds that if dancing takes place in order to excite the passions and lead to sin, this exercise is vicious and to be condemned. And that is why dances and balls cannot be regarded as an innocent and legitimate amusement.

"If a penitent who has been present at a dance did not know previously that this amusement is not allowed the confessor will act as in the case . . . in which the penitent was unaware that theatrical performances are forbidden. If he will not promise not to do so, the confessor will refuse him absolution until he does what is required and gives evidence of better dispositions."

It may be objected that, after all, this concerned a Latin country and that such objections to a common pastime would not apply to the staid manners of more northern latitudes. Yet not long after the date which now concerns us the first synod of Maynooth warned the faithful "against the improper dances which have been imported into our country from abroad to the incalculable detriment of morality and decency. Such dances have always been condemned by the pastors of the Church. This condemnation we renew and we call upon all to whom God has entrusted the care of immortal souls to use every exertion to banish from our midst what is clearly of itself an occasion of sins." Decree 216 of the same synod enjoins on all priests, secular and regular, to prevent these "fast" dances, and confessors are warned that they will not be doing their duty if on any pretext they permit such dances or excuse them.

In preaching and campaigning vigorously against dancing in his parish Abbé Vianney was not therefore without authority and he could have pointed, had he known of them, to a long list of theologians down the centuries who would have applauded his efforts. St Francis de Sales, it is true, does not condemn dancing outright, but he can hardly be said to encourage it. It is to be wondered what Abbé Vianney (or St Francis de Sales) would have made of the St Patrick's night dance that is organized on March 17, occurring usually in the middle of Lent, in many English parishes and with the parish priest's approval—even if the function is in aid of the Catholic schools. Would Abbé Vianney have refused absolution, as he did at Ars, to those who took part or merely watched the proceedings?

Preaching was not his only weapon in those early days at Ars. He used every means in his power and the confessional was one of the most powerful. At the beginning it was mostly the young women who felt this influence. Mgr Convert, quoted by Mgr Trochu, gives an account of an interview in 1895 with an old woman who told him that as late as 1835–41, when there was no longer any dancing at Ars, Abbé Vianney was still refusing absolution to dancers. Villages in the district still continued to have their annual fairs (known as *vogues*) and as a girl she was accustomed to go to that held at Misérieux nearby.

"Did you go to confession nevertheless?" Mgr Convert inquired.

"Oh, yes, for all the great feasts. M. le Curé would only give me his blessing."

"And what did he say to you?"

"'If you won't give up going to this dance you will be damned.' He was short and to the point."

Thus for six years she was unable to go to communion at Easter.

It would be easy to quote many other examples of the same sort of thing. When people from elsewhere began to come to Ars to confess to Abbé Vianney, with them he maintained the same attitude, and although on many matters he grew more indulgent, on dancing he was always adamant. At the local manor-house they had been accustomed to hold a dance for members of the family, but soon gave up the practice when they perceived their priest's attitude. There was little else that they could do when they heard words like these from the pulpit:

"Go, reprobate fathers and mothers, go to hell where God's anger awaits you, you and the fine things you have done in letting your children run wild! Go, they will not be long in joining you, since you have so clearly shown them the way! You will see if your priest was right in forbidding you these infernal joys. My God, can your eyes be so bewitched that you believe that there is no harm in this dancing, while it is in truth the cord by which the devil drags most souls to hell?"

Abbé Vianney campaigned outside the church as well as in the pulpit. He prevailed upon the mayor of the village, Antoine Mandy, to forbid public dances in the square in front of the church; on the occasion of the feast of St Sixtus (August 6), the patronal festival and the day of the annual *vogue*, some of the villagers appealed to higher authority at Trévoux and were upheld by the *sous-préfet*. When the day arrived the fair took place, therefore, and on the Sunday afternoon the young men of the village and the surrounding countryside in their best clothes made their way to the square in front of the church. What was to have been an occasion not only of enjoyment but of a decisive victory over the parish priest and the mayor did not so turn out. One or two young women servants, from neighbouring farms, were waiting there, but most of the expected partners that the young men had looked forward to were missing: the violin struck up, but with only about half a dozen people dancing the note of gaiety seemed very forced. One by one the men drifted away and the dance that was to have been the token of resounding victory fizzled out. For some reason that they did not understand the parish priest had managed to capture their partners and had taken them off to church to Vespers. By nightfall when the bell was rung for night prayers Abbé Vianney could see that victory was his.

The campaign against the taverns cost him money as well as effort. Just as on one occasion he had met the fiddler coming to play for the dance and paid him what he would have earned not to play, so also he paid the tavern-keeper not to open for the day. It was impossible for him to do this very often; nevertheless, with some of the money that came to him from his father's estate he bought out one of the taverns near the church and by dint of continual exhortations to his parishioners so deprived the others of customers that they were obliged to close their doors. As the years went by it gradually came about that the men who wanted to drink Beaujolais had to take it from their own barrel at home since there was no innkeeper for them to pay for some of his.

Sunday work, also, became a thing of the past. Abbé Vianney was hard upon that because he knew and appreciated the temptation besetting men who were at the mercy of wind and weather, who must take advantage of a sunny day to get in their crops, or a day following rain to set the young plants in the ground.

It took him ten years to effect this change in the village; at the same time women's dresses also claimed his attention. On this his notions were on a par with his attitude to dancing. Bare arms, low-necked dresses and so on were not commonly to be encoun-

tered among the women of Ars, and when in the pulpit and out of
it their parish priest delivered himself of remarks about the in-
decency of female dress it was to more harmless things that he
usually referred. He went so far as to reprove the fashion prevailing
in Ars by which women contrived to show off their hair and succeeded in persuading them to wear bonnets which, as one of them
remarked, "made us all look like old women". "For thirty years,"
Mgr Trochu remarks, "pilgrims to Ars could admire in church,
in the streets and in the country lanes the women and girls of the
village, who were 'as dignified and modest as enclosed nuns'."
If it was Abbé Vianney's ambition to make his women parishioners behave like enclosed nuns and look like old women, he was
merely trying to adopt in his parish the precepts of the saints whose
lives he read so assiduously. Women, if we listen to some of the
saints, appear as snares laid by the devil for the defenceless male,
whereas, in fact, there have been few holy men who have founded
a great work in the Church and at one time or another have not
been helped by a woman; Abbé Vianney himself owed much,
after his mother, to Mme Fayot who gave him shelter, and later
on to Catherine Lassagne who ably seconded his efforts. To set up
conventual practices as the standard for ordinary men and women
"in the world" amounts to a misunderstanding (and an unconscious denigration) of their status and dignity as lay people.

With all these efforts to achieve a moral reform of the parish,
there went on at the same time an intense endeavour to instruct
the young people and the children. It was customary at Ars, as
in other parts of the country, for catechism classes to be held
during the winter months. They were not easy children to teach,
few could read, and none was accustomed to school discipline.
The age of seven or eight saw them in the fields watching their
parents' beasts, and directly they were strong enough to wield a
hoe their laborious days began. Abbé Vianney fixed his catechism
class at six in the morning from All Saints' day until Easter. Daily
during this period he was waiting for his pupils in church, always
rewarding the first comer with some little prize as an encouragement.

He required the children to be word perfect and was strict on this point. His explanation of the day's lesson followed recitation of that of the preceding day. He showed himself as kindly, and though he could administer a telling rebuke was at pains to encourage rather than to drive. But the catechism must be learned perfectly and those whose memories failed them found their first communion postponed from one year to the next. Some were sixteen when finally they were allowed to make it. Here again Abbé Vianney was of his period, though it appears that in his literal interpretation of the law he went further than some of his colleagues, and at least one of the children of Ars, refused in his own church, was sent to Misérieux for his first communion.

Abbé Vianney inaugurated a rosary confraternity for the young women of the parish, endeavouring to train an *élite* who should be an example to others, he instituted the custom of saying night prayers every evening at 8 p.m. and he set about the embellishment of his church in order to make it attractive to the parishioners and not too unworthy of its purpose.

He had obtained a new altar soon after his arrival and during these first years in Ars often walked into Lyon in search of vestments and adornments for the church. He became known to the dealers in such things as the shabby little priest who always insisted on the best. Much of the woodwork of the church he repainted with his own hands, and two heads of angels of somewhat repulsive appearance which surmounted the altar were the fruits of one of his expeditions to Lyon. There remained, however, more considerable work to be done if the church was to become the centre of the parish and attractive to the people, for when Abbé Vianney went there first it was, to tell the truth, a miserable little building. The whitewashed walls, the pealing paint could be attended to, but to make the parish church of Ars worthy of its name more was required. The French were accustomed to refer to their village churches as *clochers* (towers); at Ars in 1820 this metonymy was inaccurate since by no stretch of the imagination could the rickety beams supporting the cracked bell be called a tower, and, in addition, they were unsafe; at any moment the bell might come tumbling down into the churchyard. In August of that year the mayor gave orders for work to be begun on a small brick tower;

two bells were to hang in it. At the same time transformation of the interior of the church proceeded apace. First a side chapel dedicated to our Lady was constructed. In 1822 the roof of the nave underwent repair, in 1823 a second chapel, dedicated to St John the Baptist, was put up: those still addicted to dancing were reminded of their parish priest's attitude to it by the inscription over the entrance to the chapel: "His head was the price of a dance."

For the time being it was the price of the chapel that worried the parish priest. He made himself responsible for the expense and owed the local carpenter five hundred francs (twenty-five pounds); he had already spent on it his salary as priest in charge of Ars, and the annual payment made by his brother François out of his share of the family estate had gone the same way. Abbé Vianney was at his wits' end; a providential gift of the amount required from an unknown woman encountered in one of the lanes some distance from the church solved his problem for him and made him resolve that in future he would pay in advance.

Mlle des Garets, the "lady of the manor", often helped Abbé Vianney with gifts for the embellishment of the church. Her brother, Vicomte François des Garets, who spent most of his time in Paris, on a visit to Ars in 1819, was captivated by the parish priest and dipped into his not inconsiderable purse on more than one occasion. In this way a canopy, a monstrance, an exposition throne, a black velvet chasuble with red orphreys for use on Good Friday, found their way to the little sacristy, though the people had to wait until 1826 before they saw the new canopy borne over the Blessed Sacrament through the village street at the Corpus Christi procession. When put together it was discovered to be too large to be carried through the church door and could not be used until the Vicomte had donated a new façade to the church and enlarged the doorway.

By 1828, when the lawn in front of the church, together with the paved approach, was completed, all seemed ready for events which were to make Ars a place of importance in the Church and known throughout the length and breadth not only of France but of the Catholic world. Yet very nearly it was not so, and had events followed their course without the intervention of the people of Ars it would have been to another village that the hordes of pilgrims travelled. Two years after his appointment to Ars word came to Abbé Vianney from the curial offices in Lyon that he was appointed to Salles, a parish of three hundred souls in the Beaujolais district with a reputation far superior to that of Ars. It was one of the "good" parishes.

With his usual simplicity Abbé Vianney loaded his possessions on a cart and set out, but finding the Saône in flood and impassable, was constrained to return to Ars for a day or two until it subsided. In the meantime a deputation from Ars hurried off to Lyon and, backed by a letter from Mlle des Garets, obtained the cancellation of the appointment. More was at stake than a change of priest: the people of the village were afraid that Ars would return to being in fact, what it was canonically, a chapel-of-ease to Misérieux, served from there and without a resident priest. Nevertheless, it is a tribute to Abbé Vianney that, despite the fulminations from the pulpit about dancing and drinking and all his efforts to reform their lives, his parishioners were not glad to see his departure and that the better elements in the parish made efforts to retain his services.

Shortly after this Ars was constituted, legally and canonically, a parish, so that Abbé Vianney achieved fixity of tenure. Thus in 1828 he was finally established. The church had been made worthier of its purpose and was filled on Sundays; on weekdays, too, it was not empty at Mass in the morning and for prayers in the evenings. Looking back over the ten years of his pastorate at Ars, Abbé Vianney had cause for satisfaction: the village was a Christian village, the worst vices had been stamped out, and though now and again he was obliged to remind his parishioners of the mortal danger of dancing—it still sometimes took place in the upper village, but never now near the church—he had not to contend with the opposition of the early years.

For this result had not been obtained without considerable personal suffering. To his penances and rigorous life must be added the difficulties of concerted opposition on the part of those parishioners particularly affected by the parish priest's reforms. He saw himself, it appears, sometimes as God's avenging angel. Speaking of anger from the pulpit one day, he told his flock that a pastor must tread human respect underfoot if he is to stamp out vice from his parish: "A pastor who would do his duty must always have a sword in his hand." Avenging angels in human form are rarely popular.

Hell was often the subject of his sermons; in the confessional refusal of absolution was by no means rare, even with children who thus found their first communion postponed for a year at least. The innkeepers, the dancers, the men who worked on Sunday all grumbled against him; taking his condemnation of their conduct as a personal matter they began to vilify him, gossiping about him and slandering him.

An unfortunate young woman living near the presbytery produced a child out of wedlock: attempts were made to spread the rumour that Abbé Vianney was the father. His true character was too well known for it to be believed, but the fact that the attempt was made caused him much unpleasantness. His extreme pallor and emaciated body were given out to be the signs of secret debauch. Rumours of all sorts were spread around the village and district. As late as 1830 the revolution of that year had its repercussions in Ars when a handful of his more unruly parishioners, encouraged by the ill-treatment of priests elsewhere, came to inform him that he must leave the village. It was an attempt that did not succeed.

Seven years previously, in 1823, the *département* of Ain was detached from the diocese of Lyon and re-established as the diocese of Belley. The new bishop, Mgr Devie, who knew nothing of Abbé Vianney, heard rumours of trouble in Ars, and received anonymous letters telling him of Abbé Vianney's scandalous conduct; he felt obliged to institute an inquiry. The parish priest of Trévoux, Abbé Vianney's dean, was sent to investigate. Of course, he found nothing whatever to substantiate the charges, but the indignity of the proceedings was an added trial to the parish priest of Ars. His reaction was typical. Twenty years later he confessed that he thought that he would be "run out" of Ars and appears to have been disappointed that his bishop did not remove him and allow him to spend the rest of his days weeping over "his poor life". He was left in Ars, he said, like a dog tied to its post.

That was not quite in accordance with the facts. A few years later, when Abbé Vianney asked to be given another parish—the reasons for this request can be examined later—the bishop offered him the more important living of Fareins where his stipend would be higher and he would have the services of a curate. Fareins was a difficult parish since of the 1,186 inhabitants upwards of five hundred of them were members of a Jansenistic sect known as *Fareinistes*. Abbé Vianney decided that this was not the sort of work he required; what he wanted was a small hidden parish somewhere where he could be forgotten, and the bishop did no more about it.

In all these trials he did not defend himself. Trials of another nature he bore too, suffering perhaps more, but saying little at the time to betray his agony. He went through a period of something like five years when he was tempted to despair of his own salvation. The obligations of a parish priest weighed heavily upon him and despite his success at Ars his duty appeared to him impossible to carry out as he ought. That he continued humbly to fulfil his obligations, never giving way to the discouragement gnawing at him, is plainly evident in his life, yet to hear him speak of his own feelings on the subject is to receive quite another impression. He was haunted by the idea of hell, he went through dreadful days and weeks and months when he felt himself abandoned by God, hopeless, damned. He was torn at the same time by acute conflict: he had to choose, it appeared to him, between the saving of his own soul by retiring to some quiet corner or peaceful monastery where he could weep over his sins, "his poor life" as he liked to call it, so getting ready to meet his Creator, and continuing to struggle along at Ars with all the fearful obligations of parish priest weighing upon him, the tremendous responsibility of the souls committed to his care. He came through this conflict as he did through others in later years, but not without their leaving a mark upon him, a scar, and provoking phenomena that were not only hard to bear but still harder for him to understand.

By 1827 it was obvious to all, even to Abbé Vianney, that the village was changed and for the better; "Ars is no longer Ars",

THE PRESBYTERY KITCHEN AT ARS

THE CONFESSIONAL FOR MEN IN THE SACRISTY

he was able to say from the pulpit. This result had been obtained by the methods which we have seen: the persevering efforts of Abbé Vianney, working on his flock, the long hours of prayer, the self-scourging, self-abnegation, and that devotion to duty which, despite his humility, was also obvious to all.

His work at Ars was successful because he was in a position to communicate to his people the truths and the precepts that it was necessary for them to know and practise. He has been given to parish priests as a model, and so it is well to realize that though his zeal and holiness are a shining example to all who follow his calling, and the ends that he pursued so earnestly are entirely praiseworthy, his methods are not necessarily to be copied. His prayer and penance were of course the basis of his life, as they should be of every priestly life, but his problems are not precisely those of the priest today.

His are different. Abbé Vianney had not the problem of communication. He not only knew his people, their problems and difficulties, he was one of them. By his origins he was a peasant, the son of a man whose kind made up the majority of his parishioners. And then he had not been formed in a seminary, to emerge after six years with a certain amount of theoretical knowledge much of which was of no practical application in parish life. It has been said of the French seminaries that they are always behind the times: in the eighteenth century they were training men to fight Protestantism, in the nineteenth "Voltairism", in the twentieth Comte, tilting against windmills long since demolished. They form men on the pattern of M. Olier's "saintly priest", but in doing so stamp them with a *cachet* that often effectively cuts them off from the concerns and life of many of their people. Good men, really holy men, perhaps, but not of the calibre of Abbé Vianney because they think in a different way, because the whole pattern of their lives and minds is frequently out of harmony with that of their parishioners. And so the working class in the countryside of France was largely lost to the Church; in the cities the working class, in so far as it was the creation of the industrial revolution, never belonged to the Church.

No doubt there were many factors contributing to this state

6

of affairs, but one of them was certainly the kind of training given to candidates for the priesthood. Men came to their parishes in the last half of the nineteenth century and the beginning of the twentieth; with enthusiasm they began to evangelize the flock committed to them, found themselves entirely separated from the lives of their parishioners with no point of insertion for their message; disheartened, if they were intellectuals they returned to their books, if they came of peasant stock they cultivated their vines or took to keeping bees. They remained faithful to their priestly obligations, estimable men, successful parish priests as the saying goes (which means that they were good administrators), but men in whom the spark was extinguished, the missionary ardour gone. And the process of extinguishing it had begun in the seminary, where they had learned an idiom that separated them from the *milieu* that they were on fire to evangelize as effectively as the walls of the seminary cut them off from the evolution of the world around them, the scene of their future labours, so that they emerged priests but men apart, outside the evolutionary demographic process going on about them. In the course of a century the working class began to grow up, but the Church failed to notice it in time, and so millions have been lost to her or millions have never known the saving message that she could bring them.

Just as a priest in a dechristianized country district, or in the non-Christian factory quarter of an industrial town of modern France, would not adopt the methods of Abbé Vianney in his work for the conversion of the flock entrusted to him, so in Ars we can hardly expect to find Abbé Vianney using the methods of today. The difference appears at once, directly we see him at work. He had not to trouble about his people's belief. He took it for granted that they were all baptized and had the faith, but the modern problem is not fundamentally a moral one, for morality in Abbé Vianney's sense is a consequence of faith. The priest today in almost every part of the world has to deal with large numbers of men and women who have never had the faith or for various reasons have given it up; ours is primarily a crisis of faith not of morals. And for that reason the priest of today cannot be uneducated as Abbé Vianney was; he must be educated at least on a par with his parishioners—and that does not mean merely the possession of a technical training which with application can be picked up in far less than the six years usually devoted to it; the whole conception of his missionary undertaking is different. He has to imbue his faithful parishioners with the idea of a worshipping community so that when converts come they can be integrated in that community, the mystical body in miniature; he has to preach the Christian mystery in all its fullness of beauty and truth, he cannot confine himself to an arid morality. There are few if any genuinely simple people to be found nowadays; the complexity of modern life has made everyone a technician to some degree, and with the progress and development of education priests will often find great numbers of their parishioners as well if not better educated than they are themselves.

The problem facing the priest is the formation of an adult Catholicism in which religious culture is on a level with, is integrated with general culture. It is a matter of opinion whether the catechism as we now have it is the best instrument for imparting knowledge of their religion to children; it is undoubted that when children are growing up and begin to encounter to the full the complexity, temptations, difficulties and considerable advantages of modern life the rudiments of the catechism are no longer sufficient if their religion is to be part and parcel of their adult life. For paradoxically it is an adult Catholicism that they need in order to grow into that state of childhood enjoined by the Gospel—become as little children said our Lord, not *be* as little children.

PART III
(1827-1859)

CHAPTER VII

OUTSIDE WORK AND THE *PROVIDENCE*

It is convenient for the sake of clarity to look on 1827 as the end of one period in Abbé Vianney's life. The following thirty-two years are very different from the time when he was working to convert his parishioners, but even then his influence was beginning to spread beyond Ars. He was known by 1827 throughout the neighbourhood as a holy priest of exceptional virtue and people from outside the parish were already coming to seek his counsel. We have seen something of the life that he led at Ars, dividing his time between his prayers, his duties in church and visiting his parishioners.

On his arrival he had charge of upwards of two hundred souls. Ten years later they numbered three hundred. For the first eight years on an average there were twelve baptisms, three marriages and five burials a year. The most conscientious of priests could have found a little spare time for legitimate recreation, spending it in gardening or reading or taking an occasional holiday.

Abbé Vianney never read a book for pleasure; apart from his professional reading, which consisted of the lives of the saints, sermons or the manual of moral theology, he read only the *Annals of the Propagation of the Faith*, and that probably only for the anecdotes that he could cull from it as illustrations for his preaching. His garden he left untouched, cutting down the fruit trees lest they prove too strong a temptation to marauding boys. He never went on a journey for the sake of recreation. The most that he allowed himself was a pilgrimage with his parishioners to our Lady of Fourvière in Lyon; anyone who has been in charge of a parish outing will know that it is certainly not a holiday.

Thus in 1823, on the patronal feast (6 August), Abbé Vianney with the majority of his parishioners, and accompanied by Abbé Martin, the priest of Savigneux, and Abbé Robert, priest of Sainte-

Euphémie, the latter nearly eighty years old, set out soon after midnight on the twenty-two mile journey to Lyon. Headed by the parish banners they walked in procession the five miles to Trévoux, singing hymns or saying the rosary. There they embarked in two large barges drawn by horses and so went slowly down the River Saône towards Lyon. On arrival at Vaise, on the outskirts of the city, they formed up in procession once more and finished the last two miles to the shrine on foot. There Abbé Vianney said Mass. The return journey by barge up the Saône was made as far as Neuville, but Abbé Vianney and one or two of his companions walked there in protest at the bad language of the men in charge of the barges. From Neuville the ten miles or so to Ars were covered on foot and in procession; the bells of the churches were rung as the pilgrims passed through the villages—Reyrieux, Toussieux, Misérieux—to reach Ars at nightfall.

All his waking hours Abbé Vianney devoted to his work and if he could not find sufficient to occupy him in his own parish he lent a helping hand to his colleagues in the district. And there was work in plenty to be done. Since the Revolution, owing to shortage of clergy, what had now once more become the diocese of Belley had very largely lain fallow; churches needed repair, their congregations needed to be brought back to the practice of religion. Many parishes had remained for long without a priest; over a period of thirty years the whole territory of the Ain *département* had only once seen its bishop, and that was in 1813, when Cardinal Fesch came from Lyon. Now with a bishop of its own, efforts were made to improve matters. Missions were given throughout the diocese, and in the corner of it which formed the deanery of Trévoux Abbé Vianney's help was needed.

The priests of the district joined forces and began with a mission at Trévoux itself which lasted nearly two months. From 9 January 1823 until a few days short of the end of February, Abbé Vianney was absent from his parish save for the week-ends when he returned for his Sunday duties. At Trévoux he did not preach but occupied a confessional which quickly became popular, so that he was in it for hours at a time. He was lodged by a M. Morel (a former fellow-pupil of his at Verrières), who on more than one occasion, after vainly awaiting him for supper, was obliged to go and seek him in church well after midnight. Apparently the leading lights of the little town came to Abbé Vianney's confessional; the *sous-préfet*, the local lawyer, the leading shopkeepers and so on. All praised his qualities as a confessor, though the *sous-préfet* admitted that he had been roundly reproved for the balls and soirées held at his official residence.

Abbé Vianney never spoke of his own achievements unless it were the means of doing good or, more commonly, he could show himself in a ridiculous light and laugh at himself. Of the Trévoux mission all he said was that the crowd nearly knocked the confessional over with the confessor inside it. Humility of this sort is attractive for it goes with a smile. He thus laughed off a successful sermon at Limas where the parish priest invited him to preach for the Forty Hours and persuaded him to come by telling him that it would only be a congregation of peasants. "The Curé played a joke on me," Abbé Vianney said later, "for when I arrived in church I found the choir filled with ecclesiastics and the nave packed with the notables of the district." Somewhat ill at ease, he began his sermon on the love of God, but warming to his subject he preached to such purpose that, in his own words, "all were in tears". But it was the joke played on him, his discomfort at getting up in the pulpit, even the somewhat odd situation of all the congregation with the tears running down their faces, the farcical nature of it all, that he stressed.

Saint-Trivier, where he was carried in exhausted after losing his way in the snow, Montmerle, where he was lodged in a private house for ten days and ate nothing but a few potatoes, Saint-Bernard, where alone he helped the parish priest and preached to such purpose that he changed the parish, all saw him for a mission or a jubilee.

He was always ready to help a colleague. A man was moved from his parish and during the vacancy Abbé Vianney looked after it; the priests at Misérieux or Villefranche were old and infirm; Abbé Vianney would come to give the last sacraments in some outlying hamlet, baptize a baby or conduct a funeral on a freezing winter's day. He returned once from Misérieux covered with mud, having lost his way in the dark. He was called out for a sick person in one of the neighbouring parishes on Sunday; leaving Ars directly after the sung Mass he walked back again for Vespers still fasting. Many were the occasions when his short night was interrupted by a sick-call that some colleague perhaps four, five or more miles away was unable to undertake. He went, always smiling, never put out, pleased to be of service. Once he arrived at Savigneux in so weak a condition that he had to be sent back in a carriage; on another occasion he arrived wet through and in high fever and was obliged to lie down while he heard the sick man's confession. He saw the ridiculous side of that: "I was in a worse state than the patient", he remarked.

As the years went on and people began to come to Ars he was hardly ever able to be absent from his confessional, and with the long hours spent in it, his short nights and spare diet, he was left, it would be thought, without much surplus energy. Yet in 1852, at the height of his arduous work and after carrying the blessed Sacrament for two hours in the Corpus Christi procession, he walked the five miles to Jassans to visit Abbé Beau, who was ill, and then made the return journey on foot again. Nevertheless, increasingly, colleagues who would see him were obliged to go to Ars. He always welcomed their visits.

"I'm glad that your good angel inspired you to come to see me," he remarked once to a priest of the district who had called.

"It's more than yours ever does," was the reply. "You never come to see me."

"I know," answered Abbé Vianney, "but then I am always busy nowadays."

*   *   *

During the first years of his pastorate Abbé Vianney had added to the work of the parish by founding an orphanage and girls' school. When he went to Ars the arrangements for teaching the children of the village were rudimentary. During the winter months a schoolmaster of sorts was procured from elsewhere and the boys and girls were taught together. This arrangement was not to Abbé Vianney's liking; he decided that there must be separate schools for the boys and girls, and soon took in hand the foundation of a school for the latter. From 1820 until 1823, during the winter months, women in the village were found who were willing to teach them, meanwhile he thought out his plans for the future and got together what money he could. In 1823 he was ready to begin by arranging for the training of his first school-mistresses. For this work he had chosen two young women, Catherine Lassagne and Benoîte Lardet, both parishioners, who though they possessed no more learning than the others in the village were of a practical turn of mind, showed sound common-sense, were obliging and kindly and devout. At the beginning of 1823 he dispatched them to Fareins, where with the nuns there they could brush up their knowledge and take their first steps in teaching children. They were there a year at Abbé Vianney's expense. Just before Easter 1824 he was able to buy, for a trifle less than a hundred pounds, a new house next door to the church; in order to do this he realized all that he could of his inheritance (his father had died in 1819) and solicited gifts for the purpose. It was not a large house: downstairs there was one large room, some thirty-six feet long by eighteen wide; upstairs two smaller rooms. That was all. It was enough, he considered, for twenty pupils.

By November the school was ready, and under Catherine and Benoîte's management it was opened as a free school for girls. Soon Jeanne-Marie Chanay from Jassans came to lend a hand as cook, washerwoman and baker for the house. Catherine Lassagne and her companions undertook courageously a by no means easy assignment. The house was to be known as the *Providence* and lived up to its name. They received no salary and often there was hardly enough to eat; very soon they were overcrowded. The three young women continued to work, living together under cramped conditions, and Catherine remained at its head for twenty-two years. Soon to the girls of the village were added those from neighbouring parishes; word had gone round that there was a good free school in Ars and parents hastened to take advantage of it.

For three years the school progressed with day girls and boarders, and then Abbé Vianney, who had been struck by the unhappy lot of many orphans in the district, sent away the boarders and transformed the institution into a combined orphanage and day school. Girls from the age of eight were received, sometimes homeless young women of sixteen or seventeen were accepted for a time; all were trained for farmwork or housework, taught sewing and cooking, and it was not long before they were in demand from the larger houses in the vicinity. If ever Abbé Vianney encountered some unfortunate girl in the district he contrived to make room for her in his beloved *Providence*. At one time there were sixty crowded into the small building, and though it had been enlarged when the orphanage was begun it was still hardly big enough for half that number. It never occurred to him to turn anyone away.

One day he brought in a girl whom he had discovered wandering homeless in the parish.

"Here," he said to Catherine, "take in this child sent you by God."

"But, Monsieur le Curé," she exclaimed, "there's no bed for her!"

"There's always yours," said Abbé Vianney, terminating the interview.

If he expected much of his helpers he gave them a good example. He was always giving away his clothes to beggars. On one occasion when he was preaching in a neighbouring parish the clergy clubbed together to get him a new pair of breeches. He put them on and started on his journey, but he never got the breeches home; he met a beggar on the way and exchanged them for his. He would walk into Lyon to beg for the *Providence*, and likely as not any money that came into his hands from other sources would be used for the same purpose. More than once he even sold some of his poor sticks of furniture when the need was great, but even these stern measures were not always sufficient. Needless to say that Abbé Vianney prayed. "I gave the saints not an instant's respite," he remarked on one occasion. But money was not always forthcoming when it was wanted.

The following incident goes back to the early years of the *Providence*, certainly before 1830. The supply of wheat, which was kept in the presbytery granary over the bedroom floor, had dwindled to a few handfuls and there was none to be had in the village owing to the poor harvest. Abbé Vianney thought that he would have to send away some of the orphans, but before doing so decided to have one last recourse to prayer. He went up to the granary, swept up what corn there was into one heap and underneath it placed a relic of St John Francis Regis, the saint who, he believed, had helped him with his initial studies for the priesthood. Then he went off to the orphans and asked them to pray. When Jeanne-Marie Chanay came up to remind him that she had nothing with which to make bread he told her to go and tidy up the granary.

When she reached the top of the ladder leading to it, it was with difficulty that she could push the door ajar. The grain was heaped up on the floor. She returned to Abbé Vianney and informed him. Together they went back and he saw that what she said was true.

The evidence for this remarkable story is better than is usually the case on occasions of this nature. It happened, it should be remembered, not five or six hundred years ago, but less than one hundred and forty. We have the evidence, given under oath, of contemporaries. We have the indirect evidence of Abbé Vianney himself. Abbé Toccanier, who acted as curate to Abbé Vianney towards the end of the latter's life, received the following account of the event from his own lips: "I had a great number of orphans to feed and in the granary there remained only a handful of wheat. It occurred to me that St Francis Regis, who had fed the poor miraculously in his own lifetime, might well do it again after his death. I possessed a relic of this saint; I placed it in among the wheat which remained, the children prayed and the granary was full." Indirect evidence comes from the bishop, Mgr Devie, who, having heard the story, at a later date when with Abbé Vianney he was in the granary turned to him and, indicating a spot on the wall, asked him point-blank:

"The grain came up to there, didn't it?"

"No, Monseigneur, higher than that," replied Abbé Vianney simply, "up to here."

Of the other extraordinary event of very much the same

nature we have better evidence still in the shape of an account, given under oath, by the person to whom it happened. It occurred, we might say, in her very hands.

Jeanne-Marie Chanay recounts how Catherine and she were very worried for the sake of the children owing to the shortage of flour and how they went off to ask Abbé Vianney to say a prayer that the flour remaining in the house would suffice. There was just enough, they calculated, for three loaves. "You must make the dough," he told them. So Jeanne-Marie began, not without a certain apprehension. She started with a very little flour and water in the kneading trough, but "I saw that my dough remained much too thick. I added water, then flour, without exhausting my small supply". Finally the trough was full of dough as it was on the days when a whole sack of flour was used and ten large loaves were baked, each weighing from twenty to twenty-two pounds.

All that they could get Abbé Vianney to say about this was, "God is very good; he looks after the poor."

That last remark was reported by Marie Filliat, who came in 1830 to take the place of Benoîte Lardet, who, to the great sorrow of Catherine Lassagne, had died that year. Marie was of a domineering nature and Catherine found her extremely trying, and increasingly so as the years went on; nevertheless, she compensated for Catherine's indulgent and kindly nature by providing the firm hand that was sometimes needed in running the orphanage. It says much for the two women that, despite their very different temperaments, they lived together after leaving the orphanage until 1882.

Abbé Vianney loved this orphanage which he had founded; he visited it every day to give a catechism lesson in the middle of the morning and this in fact was the origin of the familiar instruction which for many years was given by him in the church at Ars. It was held at first in the orphanage, and then, as people from outside began to frequent it, was transferred to the church. In the early days he would come in, wearing his cassock and surplice, a copy of the catechism in his hand, and leaning against the bread-trough, start off on the lesson immediately. He explained the day's portion in familiar language, in an idiom that could be understood by these country children. Meanwhile the three women in charge of the establishment sat by the children, occupied in sewing some garment or with their spinning. It was not unusual for the orphanage hens to wander in during the lesson.

Although the *Providence* was just behind the church, Abbé Vianney, with the bishop's encouragement, set about the construction of a small chapel attached to it. At the back of his mind was the idea, one that haunted him almost until his last years, that he would be able to retire from parish work and with no other task than the orphanage on his hands, live a life of prayer, saying Mass in the little chapel in which he intended to establish perpetual adoration. Cherished little schemes of this sort have a way of going awry, and Abbé Vianney, in spite of attempts in later years to retire to some solitude, either at the *Providence* or elsewhere, was never successful in doing so.

CHAPTER VIII

THE STRANGE AFFAIR OF THE *GRAPPIN*

FROM 1827 until his death thirty-two years later Abbé Vianney was increasingly occupied with the numerous pilgrims who came to Ars, men and women who made the journey, sometimes a very considerable journey, not to venerate a saint in a shrine, but to make contact with one whom they considered was a living saint, with the parish priest of Ars whose only shrine was the confessional, as it was his solitude, the only solitude that was granted him for all those long years. The solitude of the confessional, particularly when upwards of eighteen hours a day are passed within its narrow walls, is very real, but it was not what Abbé Vianney sought in order to prepare his "poor soul" for death.

"Ars is no longer Ars," he had said in the pulpit, nor was it, in more senses than that intended. At first people began to come to spend Sunday in the village; the church was full, there was a good attendance of parishioners and many from outside the parish were also present. "Our stay in Ars lasted until Sunday," writes one pilgrim. "On that day Mass began at eight and lasted until eleven. There was a procession before the Mass and a sermon after the Gospel." On weekdays there were generally about fifteen men and fifty women at Mass. In the space of a few years Ars had greatly changed; Jean Picard, who set up there as a blacksmith in 1832, after knowing the village in earlier years, remarks as much. Formerly the parish "was like those in the neighbourhood", but when he came back there, "owing to the parish priest, who was already hailed as a saint", the place was unrecognizable. Sunday work was a thing of the past, the men no longer drank, swore or blasphemed, the women were chaste and modest, the children instructed in their religion. All this, as we have seen, was not obtained without immense effort on the part of Abbé Vianney,

who paid for it heavily in effort, mortification and trial. One particular trial that he underwent from about 1824 until a few years
before his death has now to be mentioned; although it accompanied other and happier manifestations which enabled him to
help many in all sorts of trouble and to bring many souls back to
God, in itself it was a hindrance to him. In this chapter the facts
are given; they are fairly complete, more so indeed than in some
similar cases, particularly in the lives of the saints, though they
raise questions which do not seem to have occurred to those who
have recorded the evidence.

When, during the winter of 1824–5, he was considering the
shape that was to be taken by his *Providence*, for which he had just
bought the house, he was troubled by strange noises in the presbytery at night. It seemed as if the curtains of the bed were being
torn; he put the noise down to rats and took a pitchfork to his
bedroom the following night. The noise went on, however, despite his efforts to dislodge them, and in the morning he could see
that the curtains had suffered no harm. This continued for some
time. The second stage was reached when loud knocks were heard
on the presbytery door and shouts resounded through the rooms.
Thieves were feared—the valuables belonging to the church were
kept in a safe in the attic—and the first night Abbé Vianney got
up and went down to investigate. There was no sign of anything
unusual, but he decided not to pass the next night alone in the
presbytery and asked André Verchère to keep him company.
André was a carter, a young man of twenty-eight. The next night,
then, he kept watch, his gun loaded; Abbé Vianney had taken
the spare room, leaving his own bedroom for his guard. At about
one in the morning André, who had not fallen asleep, heard a
noise at the presbytery door as if someone trying to get in was
rattling the latch and banging on the door with a piece of wood.

"I took my gun and ran to the window," he testified, "and
flinging it open looked out. I saw nothing. The house seemed to
shake with the blows [on the door] for about a quarter of an hour.
My legs too were shaking. . . . When the noise began Abbé
Vianney lighted a lamp. He came to me.

"'Did you hear it?' he asked.

7

"'Of course I heard it,' I answered, 'since I've got up and taken my gun.'

"'And you're afraid,' insisted the Curé.

"'No, I'm not afraid,' I replied, 'but I feel my legs giving way. The presbytery is going to fall down.'

"'What do you think it is?'

"'I believe that it's the devil.'

"When the noise ceased we went back to bed. M. le Curé came back the next night to ask me to go back with him. I answered him, 'Monsieur le Curé, I have had enough of it!'"

Next Abbé Vianney asked the mayor for help; Antoine Mandy was sent to the presbytery, taking with him Jean Cotton, the gardener from the château. They slept there for nearly a fortnight, going to the presbytery after prayers had been said in church. During the whole time they heard nothing, save on one occasion when a noise "like the blade of a knife hitting a water-jug" occurred. Abbé Vianney appears to have heard something on other nights, for in the morning he asked them if they too had not heard something. On other occasions men kept watch in the church tower but heard nothing, though once they saw, it was said, "a tongue of fire which seemed to fall on the presbytery".

One night when there was snow on the ground Abbé Vianney heard a great noise "like an army of Austrians or Cossacks" all talking a language which he did not understand. He rushed down and opened the door. There was no one there and no sign of footmarks in the snow. From this time Abbé Vianney believed that he was being persecuted by the devil and no longer asked the men of the parish for protection during the night. "I believed that it was the devil because I was afraid," he told the bishop of Belley, Mgr Devie, later. "God does not make people afraid."

Abbé Vianney grew accustomed to his disturbed nights and was not always afraid. In time he became convinced that when he was especially troubled in this way a great sinner, "a really large fish" as he put it, was thus heralded for his confessional the next day. And in his playful way he nicknamed the disturber of his nights the *Grappin*. "The *Grappin's* a bit of a fool; he always lets me know when great sinners are coming!"

So for many years the raps, the knockings and the rest were continued. There were other noises. Sometimes he heard a voice crying out, "Vianney, Vianney you potato-eater! Not dead yet? I'll have you all the same!" Several times in bed Abbé Vianney felt something like a hand passing over his face or rats running over his body. On some nights there was a noise as if men were tramping about overhead. Nor were these phenomena confined to Ars.

In 1826, during a mission that took place at Montmerle, there were stories that noises had been heard from the room occupied by Abbé Vianney, and colleagues among the clergy were joking about it. Next winter he was at Saint-Trivier with other clergy for the special sermons and confession on the occasion of the jubilee. Noises were heard from his bedroom, for which his colleagues took him to task. "It's only the *Grappin*," he replied. "He's annoyed at the good being done here."

His colleagues were not convinced.

"You don't eat," they told him, "you don't sleep. It's all coming from your own head, it's the bats in your own belfry."

The following night was heard the rumble of a heavy waggon; it seemed to shake the whole presbytery. The parish priest and the others got up. A fearful noise was coming from Abbé Vianney's room, and Abbé Benoît, the curate, cried out that the Curé d'Ars was being done to death. All ran to the room, to find that Abbé Vianney was peacefully in bed, though unseen hands had pushed it out to the middle of the room.

"It's only the *Grappin*," he said with a smile. "I am sorry that you have been disturbed. It's really nothing. Though it is a good sign; we'll land a large fish tomorrow." And so it turned out. The following evening M. des Murs, a man of some importance in the village, who had not been near the confessional for years, came to ask Abbé Vianney to hear his confession.

There were other occurrences of a seemingly inexplicable nature. On occasion the bedclothes were pulled off Abbé Vianney's bed, or the bed was moved about as at Saint-Trivier. The earliest manifestation of all seems to have been in 1820, four years before the noises were first heard in the presbytery. It concerns a picture of the Annunciation which Abbé Vianney took from the church and hung in the presbytery on the corner of the stairs. One morning it was found covered with filth. All Abbé Vianney's biographers who have mentioned this incident have put it down to the work of the devil, though it seems difficult to rule out human agency, particularly as at this time Abbé Vianney was in the midst of his campaign to reform his parish and was in opposition to the dancers and drinkers, some of whom may possibly have taken this revenge upon him.

On some occasions, as we have seen, the noises were perceived by others, but generally this was not so. Abbé Raymond and Abbé Toccanier, who were both curates to Abbé Vianney, never heard a sound that was unusual. On the other hand, Gothon, his sister, who spent a night in the presbytery, heard typical *Grappin* noises just after her brother had left the house to go to church. And others heard vague rumblings, or a confused murmuring, as they walked behind Abbé Vianney up the aisle of the church to go to confession. But the evidence for this is less satisfactory than in the other instances mentioned.

At Ars today, in what was Abbé Vianney's bedroom, they show the bed that he slept in surrounded by his few possessions and the oleographs of his saints that he prized so highly. The wooden frame of the bed shows signs of burning. The fire which caused this charring of the bed was discovered when Abbé Vianney was no longer in the presbytery; he had gone to the church some five hours previously. It occurred on the morning of 23 or 24 February 1857. At about seven o'clock passers-by noticed flames and smoke coming from Abbé Vianney's room. Someone rushed to tell him just as he left the confessional to vest for Mass. He produced the key to the presbytery, remarking as he did so that it must be the *Grappin* who, unable to "catch the bird, is burning the cage". The fire was confined to the bedroom and somewhat oddly to the bed and its immediate surroundings. It seems to have gone out of itself, not penetrating to the floor above as well it might have done since the tester over the bed was near the ceiling, and stopping in the room at a point where a relic of St Philomena stood on a table. Abbé Vianney put it down, as we have seen, to the machinations of the *Grappin*; Abbé Monnin, who was present and observed the course of the fire, and how it had stopped just short of the reliquary, spoke of a miracle. And several persons in Ars at the time were disposed to agree with him.

Another explanation was put forward in a booklet published at Ars during Abbé Vianney's lifetime, though without his permission, in the year of the fire. There it is stated that the fire was caused by the match with which Abbé Vianney lighted the lantern which he always carried on his way from the presbytery to the church. The spent match may still have been glowing and having fallen among the bedclothes set them alight. They may well have smouldered for some hours before bursting into flame. In spite of Mgr Trochu's doubts on the subject—he thinks it extraordinary that a fire should smoulder for five hours, but there have been cases in which the process has gone on longer than that—this seems a likely explanation.

The incident of the fire was an isolated occasion during the last years of Abbé Vianney's life; from 1824 (from 1820 if we include the soiled picture of the Annunciation) until 1855 he endured these manifestations at night which disturbed the short sleep that he allowed himself. That at that period in connexion with a man who was reputed a saint they should have been looked on as the work of the devil seems natural enough, more especially since they occurred in circumstances and among crowds who were looking for marvels of all sorts. Abbé Vianney, too, ascribed them to the devil, though he preferred to allude to him under the pseudonym of the *Grappin*. In a later chapter of this book I offer tentatively another explanation, though in doing so there is no thought of attempting to diminish the nature of the trial that Abbé Vianney underwent. For the fact that it was a heavy one cannot be gainsaid. Indeed, the chief marvel of the whole extraordinary business is the good-humoured way in which he accepted it all, making light of it, joking about it, alluding playfully to the pranks of the *Grappin*, while all the time, at the very lowest estimate, he was being deprived of much-needed sleep. If indeed he thought that it was the devil, his conduct stands out as extremely heroic. It was characteristic of him throughout his exceptional life as a parish priest that despite trials and harder work of a more gruelling nature than has, it seems possible to say, ever been the lot of a clergyman, he could crack jokes about it. Many saints have led very busy lives, but none have gone on thirty years or more with less than three hours' sleep at night, and that broken by disturbances of an odd and unpleasant nature. How he must have longed for the days when he was curate to Abbé Balley, with a regular life and time to say his prayers!

CHAPTER IX

THE PILGRIMAGE

IF the truth be told Ars is not an attractive place. It consists merely of a winding village street with a few houses, a shop or two, an hotel of sorts, and a church to which an annexe has been added to transform it into a basilica (though anything less like the traditional basilica form from which the name is derived is hard to imagine). The street straggles on past the church, the houses grow fewer, and more scattered, and the place finally peters out on a bridge over the brook, the Fontblin, where the road as it continues its way through a wood turns almost into a cart-track. Save for the addition of houses, an improvement in the road surface in the village and the extraordinary addition to the church, the place is probably not much unlike what it was a hundred years ago.

If you go there now, save perhaps from mid-July to the end of August, you will find it quiet enough; certainly quieter than it was a hundred years ago practically at all seasons of the year. Then there were crowds every day, people milling about trying to get into the little church, trying to find a night's lodging or a meal, trying to obtain a glimpse of the parish priest, to hear him preaching or catechizing, trying to go to confession to him, to catch him as he passed and beg a blessing, trying even to snip a piece off his cassock, or filch his breviary from under his arm. The crowds gave him no peace and very little privacy. Gone were the days when with his breviary or rosary he could wander off down the road over the Fontblin and on into the woods where, under the shade of the great oaks, treading the sticky clay of his parish underfoot in his well-patched boots, he could pray in peace. The trouble was that he had put this corner of France on the map; Ars in the Dombes region of the *département* of Ain would never be the same again, and although in winter nowadays it regains its previous tranquillity, you can still feel its Curé of a hundred years ago brooding over it. And you can see what men have done to this church, and the pious trash they sell to remind you of him (*souvenirs d'Ars*) and wonder how it all began.

It happened of course gradually. And it started simply enough with former parishioners from Ecully where he had been curate, with those who had known him in Dardilly, his native village, because in both he had left a reputation for holiness. As early as 1818 he attracted people. They came, too, from Noës, where he had spent those months in hiding, eager to see "M. Jerome" as a priest, because already before his ordination they held him in veneration. Thus it was simple devout folk who came to him, and it is recorded that he preached a short retreat to some of them and that a few of them decided to remain in Ars under his direction, settled there and in letters and conversation spread his fame abroad.

In 1822 Abbé Vianney paid a visit to Abbé Loras, superior of the minor seminary at Meximieux. He had been a fellow pupil of his at Abbé Balley's and at Verrières and remained on terms of friendship with him. It was Abbé Loras who blessed the chapel of St John the Baptist at Ars in 1823. As Abbé Vianney walked across the seminary recreation ground one of the young men present—Antoine Raymond, whose name recurs again in this story: he was then sixteen—cried out, "There goes the holy Curé d'Ars!"

Very much the same sort of thing happened when he went to help his colleagues in the neighbourhood. In all the surrounding parishes the faithful flocked to his confessional and soon many of them began to make the journey to Ars to obtain his counsel. By 1827 people were coming from greater distances, and Ars saw something like twenty pilgrims a day. During the octave of Corpus Christi the young Comtesse Laure des Garets, who succeeded her aunt at the château, writing to her father remarks on the large congregation every night at benediction, among whom were to be found many strangers.

In 1828 Abbé Vianney was busy all day. People came not only for confession; curiosity was part of the attraction. He was known as a saint and they came to see this unaccustomed spectacle. Whether they made the journey for curiosity, counsel or confession, most of them went away from Ars consoled or shriven. Catherine Lassagne remarked on the phenomenon to Abbé Vianney, telling him that elsewhere missionaries sought out sinners, but "here", she said, "the sinners seek you out".

It quickly became common knowledge that Abbé Vianney could read men's consciences and he was reputed to work miracles. Certainly the extraordinary occurrences that had taken place in connexion with the *Providence*—the multiplication of the corn and the flour—were not kept secret by those who benefited by them and the news travelled fast round the countryside and further afield. Miracles are signs for those who can read them, pointing to sanctity, and very soon it was no longer consciences alone that required attention: men and women brought their diseased or ailing bodies to Abbé Vianney's attention, asking his prayers for their cure.

And cures occurred. Whether all of them would pass the strict test required in these days to establish a cure as a miracle is unimportant; many of them no doubt were due to the freeing of a conscience from a burden long heavy upon it, to the sudden passing of a condition, or a conflict, which influenced the body. In instances of this kind it is difficult to point with certainty to the instantaneous nature of a cure, particularly as the psychosomatic relation was little understood in those days. Today at Lourdes, for example, a case which was not certainly one of well-defined physical illness would not, for obvious reasons, be accepted as the basis of a miraculous cure, even though in other respects it fulfilled the conditions. Yet in one sense it seems odd that this should be so, for by a word or two of counsel, the cleansing of a conscience, a short prayer, Abbé Vianney could relieve a man of a distressing illness which nowadays might require a series of costly sessions with a psychiatrist. Technically we do not call it a miracle, but the pilgrims did, and there was no *bureau de constatation médicale* to say them nay. They came to Ars in ever-increasing numbers.

At first Abbé Vianney forbade the story of such marvels to be noised abroad. Then his attitude changed. He began to attribute all marvels that occurred at Ars to the intercession of St Philomena, a virgin martyr of the primitive Church to whom he had great devotion. That he believed in the fact of her intercession there can be no doubt at all, yet that can hardly explain the fact that it was his prayers that she answered. It was necessary to come to Ars and to inform him; he might send the petitioner to pray in the chapel of St Philomena that he had added to the church, and so the cure, or other favour, when it occurred, would be ascribed to her, and he saw to it that it was. Nevertheless his agency seemed necessary. It is hard to escape the impression that he used St Philomena as his *alibi*, thus avoiding, so he thought, the reputation of a wonder-worker. The pilgrims, though they did as they were bid, in their heart of hearts knew better.

The story of St Philomena is a strange one, though by no means unique in the annals of hagiography. She is said to be a virgin martyr of the second century, but the first that is heard of her occurs in 1802. On 24 May of that year in the catacomb of St Priscilla on the Via Salaria in Rome a *loculus* was found bearing the inscription:

LUMENA PAXTE CUM FI

together with symbolic anchor, arrow, palm and ivy leaves. The theory was propounded that the inscription was intended to read

PAX TECUM FILUMENA

("Peace be with you, Philomena"). This reading was obtained by placing at the end the tile which stood first in the inscription. It was thought that the tiles had originally been placed in the wrong order because the workman could not read or because he was in a hurry. Inside the *loculus* was the skeleton of a girl of between the ages of thirteen and fifteen, and embedded in the cement was a small glass vessel with vestiges of what was taken to be blood. In June 1805 the relics were given to Canon di Lucia, who enshrined them in the church of which he was parish priest at Mugnano in the diocese of Nola.

At this point a nun of Naples alleged that she had received revelations concerning the life of St Philomena and on this doubtful evidence Canon di Lucia produced a full-length biography.

Needless to say that on examination it proves to be entirely value-less. Nevertheless, pilgrimages were organized to the shrine, a popular cultus grew up and it is said that miracles occurred. Eventually the cultus was approved by the Congregation of Rites and a proper Mass and office were granted for the feast of St Philomena.

It seems that those who discovered the bones in the *loculus* in 1802 were far too optimistic in their conclusions and that the Congregation of Rites was misled by the experts of those days. It is well known nowadays that the "phials of blood" found in the tombs do not in fact contain blood and are no indication of martyrdom; nor are the symbols to be given the signification bestowed on them at the beginning of the nineteenth century. The anchor stands for the cross, the palm is a symbol of the reward to be obtained by all who lead a Christian life, the arrows and the leaves of ivy were placed in position to separate the words of the inscription. One reason for the jumbled inscription may well have been not mischance but design—there are other instances of the same thing—on the part of the workman; frequently in the fourth century the remains of former tombs were used again to enclose new ones, but care was taken that the original inscription should not reappear; the letters were used in their wrong order. Thus we can only conclude that the body discovered in 1802 is not that of the person mentioned by the epitaph but of an anonymous Christian girl of the fourth century. Can we assert there was a martyr whose name was Philomena? There is no proof of it; we cannot be certain that LUMENA and FI belong to the same original inscription and they could form part of many other words of which the tiles containing the remainder have been lost. In fact we hardly know any more than if the discovery of 1802 had never taken place.

Archeology has made great progress since 1802 and we cannot blame those who at the beginning of the nineteenth century interpreted the evidence as they did. Yet in spite of what is now known it is often urged that the miracles which have taken place in connexion with St Philomena "prove" the whole story. They do nothing of the sort, for in this context miracles are no historical argument; God can hear prayers as and how he wills, whatever the intermediary invoked to place them before him. That he heard Abbé Vianney's seems certain enough.

Abbé Vianney's acquaintance with St Philomena went back some years. As M. Balley's curate he had been taken by his parish priest to call on the Perrin family. Mme Perrin was the sister of Pauline Jaricot, the foundress of the Association for the Propagation of the Faith, who was devoted to St Philomena. In the *salon* of the Perrin household, from Pauline Jaricot, Abbé Vianney first heard tell of St Philomena, and from her he received a portion of the relic that she had obtained from Fr de Magallon.

St Philomena not only provided Abbé Vianney with an alibi, she became his especial saint whom he knew as his guide, consoler and friend. Abbé Monnin, who wrote the first life of Abbé Vianney, describes the relationship between the two in the following terms: "On the one side there is perpetual invocation and on the other evident assistance and in some sort a real presence". There is no doubt that the cultus of St Philomena was propagated on all sides by Abbé Vianney and that had it not been for him in all probability we should have heard little of her.

A pilgrimage is usually organized by the clergy, who urge their parishioners to travel, for example, to Lourdes, Rome or elsewhere. Nothing of the sort occurred in connexion with Ars. At the beginning, indeed, the local clergy, at any rate, were opposed to people going there and endeavoured to dissuade them from it. In spite of the good work that they themselves had witnessed in their own parishes when Abbé Vianney came to lend a hand, they gave way to their jealousy or evinced an attitude not unknown in clerical circles, namely, distrust of anything that rose above the mediocrity of their own methods and ideals. They criticized his appearance and dress, they said that he was odd (and he was, but not in the sense that they intended); they blamed him for going to meetings of the local clergymen in his old cassock and patched boots. They said that he was mean and miserly not to spend a little money on himself for a new outfit.

At a dinner presided over by the bishop at the conclusion of a mission one man remarked aloud that Abbé Vianney's cassock was unadorned by a sash.

"And he's even sitting up there with the bishop," he concluded.

"Even without a sash," replied a colleague, "the Curé d'Ars is well worth many who wear one."

"A remark to the point," added the bishop, and the conversation turned to other matters.

Although he wore old clothes and carried a battered hat under his arm, Abbé Vianney was always clean. Like St Vincent de Paul he could have said of his old cassock that it had neither holes nor stains.

Many of his colleagues remembered his rather extraordinary course of studies for the priesthood. And it was to this ignoramus, they complained, that their best parishioners were rushing off as the surest guide of conscience in the diocese. Priests stood in their pulpits and denounced this charlatan, the Curé d'Ars. Others forbade their penitents to go there under pain of refusal of absolution. They regarded it as a crying scandal that their people should go to consult a man who himself said that he knew nothing. But he also said that "those who are led by the Holy Spirit have the right ideas . . .That is why so many ignorant folk know more than men of learning." His colleagues may not have heard that remark, or if they had, did not believe that it applied to Abbé Vianney.

Yet the evidence was there for all to see. Men put difficult cases to him which he solved with ease; his decisions on questions of vocation, which seemed taken in a moment, never proved wrong, though sometimes those who consulted him, through ignorance or malice, twisted his words to suit their convenience. As always he made light of what was being said against him, pleased to be able to present himself in a ridiculous light. "Instead of the Gospel they're preaching about the Curé d'Ars now, poor man!" he once remarked. Anonymous letters began to arrive at the Ars presbytery.

"You are said to be a saint," one ran, "and yet everyone who goes to see you is not converted. You would do better to moderate your ill-judged zeal, otherwise we shall be obliged, though with regret, to inform the bishop."

Abbé Vianney recognized the hand of one of his colleagues.

"Monsieur le Curé," he replied, "I thank you sincerely for the charitable advice that you have been good enough to offer me. I acknowledge my ignorance and my incapability. If people from neighbouring parishes have not been converted after receiving the sacraments at my hands I am indeed deeply sorry for it. If you think it a good thing you can write to the bishop who, I hope, will be kind enough to move me. . . . Please pray to God that I do less evil and more good. . . ."

Some of the clergy sent out a circular letter to their colleagues intended to be sent on to the bishop in denunciation of Abbé Vianney. A copy of the document came into his hands; he signed his name on it and despatched it to the bishop, remarking, "Now they have my signature, the evidence against the culprit is complete."

A last instance of the sort of opposition with which he had to contend is provided by the behaviour of Abbé Borjon, who in 1837 was appointed parish priest of Ambérieux. He was under thirty at the time and his inexperience, coupled with a certain brusqueness of manner and self-sufficiency—he was one of those who pride themselves on their plain speaking—did not make him well loved by his new parishioners. Some of them had offended him by offering him a stipend to celebrate a Mass for their intention; only afterwards did he discover that their intention was his removal from the parish and replacement by Abbé Vianney. When, in addition, he found that some of them, under Abbé Vianney's direction, had established some sort of confraternity at Ars and had been collecting money for it in his own parish of Ambérieux, he was very angry. He sat down at once and wrote to Ars a letter expressing his anger, and telling the culprit that men with so little theology had no right to set foot inside the confessional.

Abbé Vianney took his pen and replied. In that spidery writing with more than one blot on the page and spelling mistakes—he never was able to spell properly—he sent back an answer that touched the heart of his correspondent.

"I have every reason to love you," he told him, "for you are the only one who really knows me. Since you are so kind and charitable as to take an interest in my poor soul please help me to

SPECIMEN OF ABBÉ VIANNEY'S HANDWRITING: PART OF A LETTER TO HIS BISHOP obtain the favour that I have been asking for a long time past so that, being moved from a post for which I am unworthy on account of my ignorance, I can retire to some corner to weep over my poor life. I have much penance and expiation to perform, many tears to shed. . . ." And he really meant it. Abbé Borjon read the sincerity of those lines and hastened to Ars to ask forgiveness; he always afterwards held Abbé Vianney in high esteem, giving evidence for the beatification to that effect.

The opposition was not continual, hard trial though it was at the times when it occurred. And the bishop was well informed of the real state of affairs at Ars. Reports and complaints had reached him at Belley and finally he had sent Canon Ruivet, his vicar-general, to investigate. Abbé Vianney informed him that he sought out no one, but that when penitents came to him he did what he could for them as his conscience directed him, but that he felt his position as parish priest a heavy burden and had already petitioned the bishop to be freed from it.

In fact he hoped for much from this episcopal investigation and was disappointed to overhear Canon Ruivet remark that if the charges against Abbé Vianney were true there would not be the crowd of pilgrims, including priests and religious. All that the bishop did, on receiving an entirely favourable report, was to invite Abbé Vianney to submit to the episopal council the difficult cases that he encountered in his work, together with his own proposed solution. In the course of a few years two hundred such cases were sent in and with none of Abbé Vianney's solutions was there found cause for disagreement.

*　　　*　　　*

The last time that Abbé Vianney was able to absent himself from Ars for the diocesan retreat was in 1834. Then, as a mark of official approval, the bishop designated him as one of the official confessors. His colleagues crowded to his confessional, yet it cannot have been anything like his day's work at Ars where he was in the confessional anything from sixteen to eighteen hours a day. From the trickle of twenty persons a day in 1827 the flood of pilgrims had swollen by 1845 to three or four hundred a day. In the last year of Abbé Vianney's life there must have been something like one hundred and twenty thousand who made the journey to Ars.

How did they get there? They made the journey on foot a few of them, the country people from the surrounding district and from as far as sixty or eighty miles away. Others came in their own coaches. By far the greater number used the available public transport. Two horse-drawn omnibuses a day travelled from Lyon to Ars, and two others connected with the Paris–Lyon railway service at Villefranche; another omnibus plying between Villefranche and Villars stopped at Ars. At the booking office at the Lyon–Perrache station a special window was in service for issuing tickets to Ars—special tickets valid for eight days, for it was known that one could not hope to go to confession to Abbé Vianney in under three days.

Five houses in Ars bore the name of hotel, but they could lodge only a fraction of the pilgrims, and the villagers at a small price gave bed and board to many more. A number of shops and stalls provided the pilgrims with candles to burn at the shrine of St Philomena, rosaries for the Curé's blessing and pictures of him. These latter were not sold with his approval, and generally, if he could get his hands on one, he tore it up. Nor were they a good likeness. There were small prayer-book cards and large oleographs of vivid frightening colours depicting scenes from his life wherein much imagination made do for little information.

During those years at Ars there were crowds everywhere, in the streets and in church, but they were well-behaved crowds. In the church particularly there were long lines of waiting penitents all day long. They only left the building when it was closed at night, and returned in the early morning directly Abbé Vianney opened it again after his short rest. Many in order not to lose their turn passed the few hours that elapsed between one day and the next in the porch of the church; during the day those who could not endure the long wait in church—freezing cold in winter and suffocating in summer—paid some poor person to keep their place. Abbé Vianney dealt with them all in rotation, the men in the

8

sacristy, the women in the confessional in the chapel of St John the Baptist. He was quick in the confessional, listened to the accusations, gave a very few words of advice always to the point, and absolution. He could not waste a minute, but he always gave the time required to each penitent.

With some he was short. A woman from Grenoble asked him if she should establish a café in order to provide for the education of her daughters, "Ask your parish priest" was the reply. On rare occasions he refused to hear a penitent who, he foresaw, had come with the wrong motives—those, for example, who intended to return to their homes and boast of the revelations made to them by the Curé d'Ars—and sent them away at once. One rather odd woman he told to go away and asked the beadle to see that she left the church. "Deliver me from this woman," he remarked calmly, "see that she goes out. She is to be pitied."

Vocations were decided, conversions effected, cures performed. It would be tedious to give numerous examples for in all cases there is a sameness about the recital that is inevitable; it is the personal factor, to be involved oneself or to know someone who has undergone an experience of the sort, that can really bring home the extraordinary nature of what went on at Ars. And at this distance of time that is impossible, though there might still be found those who have spoken with men and women who made the pilgrimage at Ars before 1859. The following examples of Abbé Vianney's work of healing souls and bodies are a very small sample of the hundreds of cases that have been recorded in detail.

A priest who felt drawn to the religious life asked Abbé Vianney in confession if he should continue to entertain this idea of giving up his work in a school and entering a monastic order.

"The desire comes from God, my friend," was the reply. "You are right to entertain it."

"So you allow me to give up my post and become a monk."

"You go too fast. You must stay where you are. God sometimes gives us desires which are not to be realized in this world."

Many were disappointed at the ordinary nature of his advice on many occasions. It hardly seemed worthwhile making the journey to Ars to be told that one must do one's duty. In the confessional he gave evidence of wisdom out of the ordinary and it was precisely in cases of real sinners that this was to be seen. But there was also an intuition that seemed supernatural.

A young man of Villefranche went with some companions to Ars, but in order to show that he had nothing to do with the pilgrimage carried his gun and took with him his dog as if he were out for a day's shooting.

"I don't mind going to have a look at this wonder-working Curé of yours," he told his companions, "but that will be all. Afterwards I shall be able to shoot a wild duck or two for the pot. You go to confession if you like."

The party arrived in Ars just as Abbé Vianney was coming out of church at midday. They stood among the line of pilgrims who always besieged him at this moment. He came forward slowly, blessing those in his path, and then stopped before the young man with his dog.

"It's a pity your soul is not so fine as your dog," he remarked.

The young man was embarrassed and bent his head. But that simple remark caused him to think furiously. It had touched off something in his soul that he had not previously suspected to be present. After a long struggle within himself he decided that the wild duck could wait; leaving his gun and his dog in the porch he pushed his way into the church. At last his turn came and he was called into the sacristy. He made his confession and was absolved. But Abbé Vianney had not done with him. As it had all begun, so it ended, with a short remark out of the blue.

"You must become a Trappist," concluded Abbé Vianney.

The vocation thus summarily decided proved in the event to be a genuine one. The young man was admitted at the abbey of Aiguebelle and lived there for thirty-six years as Brother Arsène. He died in 1888.

Then there was the geologist of Lyon, M. Maissiat, whose amiable habit it was to call himself a philosopher, meaning thereby that he believed nothing that could not be proved to him by reason. He had been brought up as a Catholic and made his first communion during the time of the Terror but gave up his religion in order to become a Mahommedan; still not satisfied, he tried Judaism, Protestantism, Spiritism and finally Communism. His reason had certainly led him on strange journeys.

In June 1841 he left Lyon for a holiday in the hills of Beaujolais and by chance encountered in the coach a friend who told him that he was on the way to Ars. M. Maissiat allowed himself to be persuaded to visit the place, though he made it clear that he had no belief in miracles such as his friend promised him that he would see. He spent the night in Ars, and the next morning, impelled by his curiosity, was present in the church. On the way to the altar Abbé Vianney caught the sceptic's eye and after Mass came up to him, put a hand on his shoulder and directed him to follow him into the sacristy. On arrival there he was told to kneel and make his confession. He refused. Abbé Vianney continued to hold his gaze. M. Maissiat knelt. Even if I do confess, he thought, it will not matter..It does not mean anything and no one will ever know about it. So, just to satisfy this importunate priest, he rattled off all the sins of his life that he could remember. Abbé Vianney listened, but was not deceived.

"Come back to me tomorrow, my friend," he concluded the interview. "In the meantime go to St Philomena's altar and ask her to pray to God for your conversion."

M. Maissiat did as he was bid. Standing before the altar, still in the same frame of mind, he suddenly discovered that the tears were rolling down his face. Finally he ran weeping out of the church. Next morning he was in the sacristy again, but with dispositions that were entirely different.

"Father," he began, "I believe in nothing. Help me." Though he did not realize it, Abbé Vianney had already helped him. Grace was at work. For nine days more he stayed in Ars, listening to the sermons, joining in the prayers, and seeing his confessor. He returned to Lyon and persevered in his religion to the end. There are many other cases of the same kind.

For thousands Abbé Vianney was a voice in the confessional in St John the Baptist's chapel, or a shrunken figure in a chair with high arm-rests in the sacristy. A voice of few words more often than not, but every one of them told. As he grew older the severity of his earlier years as a priest diminished. He learned that there was another, and more approved, school besides that of Mgr Joly de Choin and his *Rituel de Toulon*. Abbé Raymond, who helped him at Ars for some time, procured for him Gousset's French translation and adaptation of St Alphonsus's moral theology—*Théologie morale à l'usage des curés et des confesseurs*. His copy was published in 1845, but before that, as early as 1840, he acted on the counsel that he received from fellow priests, notably from the diocesan missioners, and no longer, save in very exceptional cases, deferred absolution for long periods.

His work as a confessor was distinguished not only by the conversions that he effected but by the extraordinary insight that he had into men's minds. At times when the crowds were even heavier than usual he would bless a penitent and send him or her away, saying that his services were not needed. The Cardinal Archbishop of Malines brought his niece, Mlle Claire Deschamps, to Ars in January 1853 for advice about her vocation. Abbé Vianney sketched a sign of the cross over her, saying as he did so, "Yes, my daughter, the community of the Sacred Heart is your vocation. You do not need absolution before communicating this morning." And that was all. With others he was longer. He would help them to examine their consciences and showed knowledge of sins that they had forgotten. Dialogues like the following, which occurred in 1841, were not uncommon.

"I was last at confession something like ten years ago."

"A bit more, wasn't it?"

"Twelve . . ."

"Still a bit more?"

"Why, yes, the last time was the Jubilee of 1826."

The conversion of sinners was Abbé Vianney's constant prayer and the intention behind all his mortification and hard work. He was once asked if he had the choice of remaining on earth to continue his work or of going to heaven which he would choose. "If I were given the choice I would remain until the end of the world," he replied. That remark is often attributed also to Charles de Foucauld, but Abbé Vianney made it first. He also said it would never be known in this world how many sinners found their salvation at Ars, yet he took no credit on himself for the work that was done. "Although I am only an ignorant priest," he added, "God who has need of no one makes use of me for this great work; if there were a more suitable instrument ready he would have made use of it and the work would have been done a hundred times better."

Sinners sought him out. With them his task was easy. Others he approached in the church when they least expected it. Having come to Ars to please a friend or from curiosity, they found themselves singled out and taken to the confessional. Still unwilling, they would find some sin of their past revealed, some circumstance or habit that they were unwilling to give up, known to this extraordinary priest. A single remark, trite enough if put down in cold print, because it lacks the personality behind it, might sometimes change a man's life. One unwilling penitent exclaimed in the confessional, "Why are you weeping, Father?" "Because you do not weep, my son," was the rejoinder. No more exhortation was necessary.

Occasionally with a full church awaiting him for confession Abbé Vianney would come out of the confessional and sign to someone waiting near the door. It might be a mother of a large family who had no time to wait, it might be a man who had looked in out of curiosity. Abbé Vianney always seemed to know on these occasions. And he was careful not to keep his own parishioners waiting; he always gave them first call on his time.

His mission was the conversion of sinners, and like many saints before him right back to the time of the Gospel, the gift of healing the sick was combined with it. Healing the body was the sign of the healing of the soul that took place at Ars. Little children seem to have been especially favoured at Ars. Yet he always appears to have been embarrassed by a cure and all the commotion that it caused and towards the end of his life he prayed for the cures to cease. Ascribe them as he might to St Philomena, people were always too inclined to allot him a part in the proceedings. Abbé Toccanier questioned him about this.

"Do you know, Monsieur le Curé," he inquired one day, "that people are saying that you have forbidden St Philomena to work any more miracles?"

"It is true," he replied; "all that caused far too much talk and brought too many people here. I told her to convert their souls but to heal their bodies after their departure. And she has done what I said. Many people have begun their novena here and been cured at home without fuss."

There were cures and conversions at Ars. People came also for consolation in great sorrow, in trouble, in bereavement. For all these he had a word of help which was effective. In addition there seems no doubt that he predicted accurately the course of events in certain lives. Since his death many prophecies have been attributed to him, but so far as can be ascertained they are all false; they concerned public events, such as the war of 1914–18, and about such things he never spoke; he confined himself to the lives of private individuals. Thus he prevented a young woman from entering a convent which, in his view, would be closed in a year. And so in the event it turned out. But most of his predictions related to the conversion of sinners and the spiritual guidance which he gave to many.

The faculty of seeing material things at a distance is less uncommon than prediction of the future and one almost expects to find examples of it in Ars. A young man from Lyon had hardly arrived in Ars when Abbé Vianney picked him out of the crowd to tell him that he must return home quickly because his house was on fire. A country woman was told after her confession that there was a serpent in her house. She hurried home and searched to no purpose. At length she thought of shaking out the mattress which during her absence had been placed in the sunlight to air; from it crawled a long snake. These instances are just two taken from among a large number; viewed in isolation they are no more remarkable than the phenomena that can be produced on occasion by clairvoyants, but taken in conjunction with the other phenomena that we have considered they add one more detail to an extraordinary picture.

*   *   *

It seems difficult to conceive how Abbé Vianney managed to crowd into a day not only the many hours spent in the confessional, the interviews outside it, and all the various demands on him occasioned by the pilgrimage, but also the necessary amount of sleep, the time for food and his priestly duties, the divine office and Mass. If we examine the pattern of a typical day in his life when the pilgrimage was at its height, between, say, 1845 and 1859, we can see how he managed to do all that he did, but at the same time we have to bear in mind that such a day was typical of every day and that long before 1845, as early perhaps as 1830, this was the daily pattern of his existence. What a man might do occasionally, if put to it to find time for urgent work, Abbé Vianney did every day for something like thirty years. It seems surprising that he did not die of exhaustion long before 1859.

His day began at one in the morning. Just before that hour his flickering lantern could be discerned as he made his way across the courtyard that separated church from presbytery; shortly afterwards the angelus rang out, informing the parish and the pilgrims that Abbé Vianney was in church awaiting penitents. He would have found a certain number of them standing near the church or in the porch. After kneeling on the altar step for a little while he went off to the confessional in the chapel of St John the Baptist. There he heard the women's confessions until six in summer and seven in winter. It was then that he said Mass. Even while he was vesting, the pilgrims could not leave him in peace; men would be arguing about who should serve his Mass, others, men and women, came to ask his prayers for their intention. He acknowledged their requests by an inclination of the head. He said Mass, we are told, with recollection and concentration to a degree that made him a model for all to follow, but on an average he never exceeded half an hour. He carried out the ceremonies naturally and carefully; there was no idiosyncrasy about him in this matter save in one respect. In the Lyon use, which he followed all his life—the diocese of Belley adopted the usual form of the Roman rite in 1867—the celebrant is required to stretch out his arms in the form of a cross during the prayer *Unde et memores*. Abbé Vianney did so for a longer period than that ordered by the rubrics. After Mass he put on his rochet and stole and went to kneel before the altar. Here once more he was allowed no peace. Pilgrims came up to look at him, they would approach closely

and stare, and went so far, sometimes, as to make remarks about
him. When he had finished his thanksgiving he returned to the
sacristy, where a heap of medals, rosaries and objects of devotion
were placed for his blessing and a pile of religious pictures awaited
his signature. A sign of the cross over the heap to be blessed, his
initials scratched at the foot of the pictures (*J.M.B.V. Curé*, was
his usual method of signing), a word or two to those who came
at this time to obtain his advice, and he hastened off to the *Providence* for the cup of milk ordered by the doctor after his illness
of 1827. He was soon back again and established in the confessional in the sacristy where the men were queueing up to go
to him.

At ten he managed to leave the penitents for a little while he
knelt on the sacristy floor and said the Little Hours of the breviary. He then returned to the men's confessions until eleven
o'clock when he went down into the church to give the catechism
lesson from a small pulpit specially reserved for the purpose.
These lessons took the place of those previously given at the
Providence.

It was a familiar instruction, given with the utmost simplicity
of form and matter. He would read out one or two questions and
answers from the catechism, and then, laying the book aside, he
started on the explanation. Possibly he would not remember for
long the particular point under consideration, and a slight digression would lead him naturally to his favourite topic, the love of
God. Some of his remarks on these occasions have been written
down, but it has been impossible to record the tone of voice, the
facial expression with which they were uttered; repeated in cold
print they seem to take on a banality that makes it difficult to
account for the effect that his simple words achieved.

"The more one knows of men the less one loves them, but with
God it is the precise contrary; the better he is known, the better he
is loved. . . . . The knowledge of God enkindles such great love
in the soul that it cannot love or desire anything outside him.
Man was created by love, that is why he is so carried away by it.
Yet he is so great that nothing on earth is enough for him. It is
only when he turns to God that he is satisfied. If you take a fish

from its water it will die. You see: so it is with man without God. . . .

"Earth is a bridge on which to cross the water; it serves no other purpose than a place on which to stand. . . .We are in the world, but not of the world, since we say every day, 'Our Father, who art in heaven'.

"A pure soul is like a fine pearl. As long as it is hidden in a shell in the depths of the sea, no one thinks of admiring it, but when it is exposed to the light of day this pearl shines, it attracts attention. It is thus that a pure soul now hidden from the eyes of the world will one day shine before the angels in the light of eternity."

Sometimes many of those present could not hear what he said, or could not understand, but in some extraordinary way the words told nonetheless. Perhaps it was the sight of him, the knowledge of what he was, his gentle smiling face that touched men's hearts. The congregation was a very mixed one. Priests and nuns, peasants, people of importance from all over the world rubbed elbows in the little chuch. Sometimes a bishop was to be found among them. Abbé Vianney referred in a catechism lesson to one who had been there.

"Because our Lord does not let himself appear in all his majesty in the most holy Sacrament of the altar you behave without reverence, but it is he nonetheless. He is in the midst of you . . . like the good bishop who was here the other day! Everyone jostled him, but if they had known he was a bishop they would have behaved better towards him."

Sitting at his ease, resting against the rail of the small pulpit, in his long rochet and wearing a black *rabat* with its white piping, sometimes wagging an admonitory finger but generally sparing of gesture, a fleeting whimsical smile on his face, he gave these simple instructions without preparation—he had no time to prepare them—with no affectation or trick of oratory, and in his simplicity converted hundreds. A passing remark, the expression of his countenance, a sigh at the mention of sin, often sufficed to change a man's whole life. He repeated himself, he spoke in familiar language, sometimes he wept, but all that he did so artlessly was supremely effective.

At midday, kneeling before the altar, he said the Angelus and then left the church to take his midday meal. In practice it was not as simple as that and sometimes the dozen yards from the church to the presbytery took him a quarter of an hour, for the way was lined on either side by pilgrims who wanted a blessing, a mother with a sick child to be healed, a cripple to be cured. They pushed and jostled, awaiting his appearance at the church door. Directly he was seen coming through the door there was a moment's silence as he let his eyes fall on them, embracing the whole crowd with a glance. Then the babel broke out.

"Holy father, bless me!"

"Pray for my son!"

"Cure this poor little child!"

"Convert my husband!"

He could not reply to all. With a word here and there, he started to make his way across to the presbytery, laying his hands sometimes on a child's head, answering a request for prayers with the gesture of a finger pointing to heaven, consoling a poor woman with a few words: "Your husband is saved, but you must pray for him."

At last he was at the presbytery door and all that remained was for him to get through it alone; he kept this one hour of the day for himself. Sometimes when the crowd pressed round him he would take a handful of medals from his pocket and scatter them among them, slipping through the door and locking it behind him while attention was thus momentarily distracted.

In the presbytery he would find his meal awaiting him. It was prepared at the *Providence* and left ready for him on the table. On the bare wood was an earthenware plate containing the meagre ration that he allowed himself: a few vegetables, two eggs sometimes, very occasionally a little meat if he were particularly exhausted, but this latter he never took without previously asking permission from his confessor. A jug of water, a bottle of red wine and piece of bread formed the complement of this modest meal. He ate quickly and managed to dispatch what he required in less than ten minutes, never sitting to do so, never finishing all that was provided. He drank a little water which he coloured with a drop of wine, he nibbled at the bread, but there was always a considerable amount of the meal left on the plate when he had finished. A pound of bread would last him a week.

The truth was that he was unable to eat more than he did. Long training and much suffering, the years of what he called his "youthful follies", when he managed to exist on a few mouldy potatoes and a crust of bread, followed by a long period of eating very little (though under medical advice his diet was less rudimentary), had allowed his stomach so to contract that he could not eat more without harmful effects. When the bishop came to Ars, on one occasion he was entertained at the château and desired Abbé Vianney's presence at dinner, which was one of the kind usually offered to bishops. He insisted that his "dear Curé", as he called him, should behave like other people and eat a proper meal. Abbé Vianney did so and afterwards very nearly died of the resulting indigestion. After that, one is glad to know, the bishop left him alone.

Five minutes, at most ten, for his dinner, a few more minutes, ten perhaps, of sleep, and he was off to visit the sick of the parish, including any pilgrims confined to bed in one of the houses of the village. Certainly his "dinner hour" (from midday to one) was well filled—"between midday and one o'clock I've managed to have dinner, sweep my room, shave and sleep and visit the sick", he once explained to a questioner.

Up to 1845 he performed single-handed all his duties of parish priest; after that date he had an assistant to whom he relinquished all the parochial work save the sick, whom he visited regularly. Sometimes the very ill would come to Ars to finish their days with Abbé Vianney's blessing, and there were others who hoped for a cure. Once again he had to make his way through the crowds who were awaiting his emergence from the presbytery door. Two or three men, volunteers for the task, made a way for him through the throng. People knelt in his path, imploring a blessing, asking for a rosary or a medal that, it was known, he carried in his pockets. In this way a little girl from Lyon managed in three days to obtain a number of medals. On the last day as Abbé Vianney pressed one into her hand he remarked on the fact.

CORRECTLY

"My child," he said, "that makes seventeen!"

Counting up her booty afterwards she discovered that the total was correct. Sometimes the supply ran out. Two brothers of the name of Lémann, converts from Judaism, asked him for medals as he was returning from visiting a sick man on the borders of the parish . . . There were none left in his pockets. Smilingly, he crossed the road to a shop, demanded a gross of medals, blessed them, and gave a handful to each of the brothers.

"Ask anyone here to pay for them," he added to the shop-keeper as he made his way back to the church.

Whenever he could manage it he made a point of calling at the *Providence* to see the children, if only for a moment or two. During the last six years of his life the room next to the chapel at the orphanage was used for the curate and visiting clergy. Abbé Vianney would drop in as they were finishing dinner and talk for a few moments—joking and sometimes teasing them gently. They would urge him to have some dessert or a glass of wine, but all that he would take, and that only rarely, was a cup of sugarless coffee which, he said, he found exceedingly bitter.

It was now one o'clock or after and his penitents awaited him. Back in the church once more he finished the day's office saying Vespers and Compline, kneeling on the stone floor in front of the high altar, and then went straight to the confessional where he heard the women. At five o'clock he moved to the sacristy to deal with the men and remained there until nearly eight o'clock when he said night prayers from the pulpit for the assembled congregation. This done he went across to the presbytery where, possibly, further interviews awaited him: visiting clergy, his curate, the brothers who had come to work in the parish, took this opportunity of a word with him and might keep him half an hour or even an hour. At last he was able to go up to his room.

There he said Matins and Lauds of the next day and read a little of the lives of the saints. And now he could go to bed, but in all likelihood it was not to sleep. If in later years he was no longer troubled by the *Grappin* the state of combined exhaustion and nervous excitation prevented his obtaining the full benefit of the scanty hours that he allowed himself. He was prone to a trouble-some cough which obliged him to sit up in bed, often several times in the hour, but above all he was a prey to all the human misery, the sins and conflicts of all sorts and conditions, which were poured into his ears throughout the greater part of his long day. The burden weighed heavy upon him. And he was unable to indulge his longing for solitude and prayer. Alone in his room, when sleep did not come, his flickering light showed him the pictures of his favourite saints hanging on the wall. He thought of them and how their whole existence was now wrapped up in God, and longed not for his release but for solitude, a monastic cell, a hermitage where he could begin to prepare "his poor soul" for death. He was unable even to attend the annual clergy retreat. In 1835 he had presented himself at the seminary at Brou only to be told by the bishop that his presence was unnecessary.

"You don't need a retreat," said the bishop, "but sinners need you in Ars." And back he was obliged to go.

So the short night passed. However bad it proved, however little sleep he managed to obtain, punctually at one o'clock the Angelus rang out—earlier sometimes, even at midnight, if the crowd of penitents was exceptionally great—and all the village and its hundreds of pilgrims knew that Abbé Vianney was back in his confessional.

CHAPTER X

ABBÉ VIANNEY'S NEW CURATE

IN 1843 Abbé Vianney was fifty-seven. The kind of life that he had led for the previous twenty-five years had not been one to benefit his health and for some time past he had been feeling the effects of his early imprudences. Severe toothache, facial neuralgia and attacks of acute colic were of frequent occurrence; despite such painful reminders of his body he treated it no better and carried on his work practically unaided. As early as 1834 the parish council had written to the bishop asking for a curate, but there was no one to spare and all the bishop could do was to urge neighbouring priests to lend a hand when occasion offered. Abbé Tailhades spent the winter of 1839-40 at Ars, Abbé Derognat, parish priest of Rancé, sometimes came to help. Abbé Raymond, of Savigneux, after the winter of 1842, began to spend more time in Ars than in his own parish, and was finally appointed to Ars as assistant.

There is no doubt that he held Abbé Vianney in high esteem, but he was one of those men who like to manage everything that they encounter; he seemed to consider that he could do everything far better himself. He felt that the pilgrimage to Ars, for example, needed organizing; if it were put on a businesslike footing, with appropriate rules and regulations, it would be far more efficient: charity would benefit, for instead of the contributions of the faithful being left to Abbé Vianney's haphazard methods—he seemed to give away all that he received no sooner than he had it in his possession—Abbé Raymond would husband it and employ it for the good of the Church and in furtherance of properly organized works of mercy. The crowds could be dealt with more efficiently. Ars, rightly handled, could be a pilgrimage centre that was the admiration of the Catholic world. Abbé Vianney with all his virtues was far too happy-go-lucky and gave way excessively to the importunity of the crowds; he seemed to have no idea what benefits would result from the plans that were maturing in Abbé Raymond's head.

In thinking thus Abbé Raymond showed his utter lack of understanding of the whole phenomenon of the Ars pilgrimage. How could he have failed to realize, we ask in our astonishment, that the pilgrimage was concerned exclusively with Abbé Vianney; that without him it was nothing? Yet undoubtedly Abbé Raymond encouraged him to entertain desires of retirement, and on one occasion assisted him to leave the parish. For what end? So that he, Abbé Raymond, should secure the appointment as parish priest of Ars. Incredible as it sounds, that really was the cherished plan that was forming in his mind.

Events played into his hands almost from the beginning of his association with Ars. In May 1843, Abbé Vianney fell ill. For some sixteen years it had been his custom to conduct the May devotions himself instead of obtaining a special preacher for the purpose. Every night from the pulpit he would read a passage from a suitable book and afterwards comment upon it, usually at length: "Once started off," writes Catherine Lassagne, "he spoke for some time." On May 3 he went up into the pulpit and began to read from the book, but it was seen that he was gasping for breath and could not continue. He knelt down to say the customary prayer and could scarcely get out the first few words. Obviously he was very ill. Willing hands carried him to the presbytery and laid him down on Abbé Balley's bed. Comte des Garets came from the château bringing a better mattress, Dr Saunier, summoned in haste, diagnosed pneumonia. As the patient's condition grew worse three other doctors were called in consultation. Abbé Vianney's pulse was very weak, his breathing laboured. Gravely the doctors decided that he was to be kept quiet. He knew that he was very ill, but once again the comic side of the situation struck him. They had forbidden him to speak but he managed to gasp out a few words.

"I'm fighting a great battle . . ." he said.

"Against whom?" they inquired, thinking no doubt of the forces of evil arrayed against the soul of this holy priest.

"Why, against four doctors. If a fifth comes it's all up with me!'

Yet devils and hell were very present to his mind. He acknowledged that he would like to live a little longer to atone for his sins
and do some good at last. He was feverish and restless, troubled by
nightmares of hell. He endured all with patience, doing as he was
told and never complaining. The pilgrims hardly knew where to
turn. The sick man's room was forbidden them and they felt no
desire to accept the ministrations of the good priest—Abbé Lacôte
—who was in charge for the time being, nor of Abbé Raymond,
who was doing what he could to lend a hand; all that they could
think of was to send up basket after basket, each full of medals,
beads and pictures for Abbé Vianney's blessing. It was generally
accepted that he would die and they took this last chance of
obtaining something from him if it was only his blessing on a
medal.

There was no longer the crowd around the confessional, all
were before the altar of St Philomena burning candles and praying
for the confessor. By 11 May Abbé Vianney seemed at the point
of death and was not expected to last more than a few hours. A
novena of Masses was begun. In the evening seven priests were
gathered round the bedside of the dying man and it was decided
to administer the last sacraments, but to spare the pilgrims and the
parishioners the dismay such news would cause, the bell was not
to be rung. But Abbé Vianney insisted.

"A parish priest has great need of the prayers of all," he said.

Immediately there was a rush for the presbytery. Pilgrims and
parishioners stood on the staircase and were massed in front of the
door. Abbé Vianney was anointed and received viaticum with
devotion. When all had left his bedside save Abbé Dubuois, the
priest of Fareins, he promised to have a hundred Masses celebrated
in honour of St Philomena and asked that a large candle should be
set up to burn at her shrine. Thereupon he appeared to fall into a
coma. Dr Saunier came in and felt his pulse. He gave him an hour
to live at the most. Shortly afterwards Abbé Vianney seemed to
rally, opened his eyes and managed to speak; for three hours he
lay there apparently calm, and then a sudden rise in temperature
dashed the onlookers' hopes once more. It was decided that if the

9

patient lasted through the night the first of the Masses in honour
of St Philomena would be celebrated in the morning.

Next morning, since Abbé Vianney was still breathing, Abbé
Dubuois celebrated Mass at the altar of St Philomena before a
congregation that crowded all the available space in the little
church. While this was going on Abbé Vianney was in a great
state of agitation, very feverish and obviously in great mental
anguish. The schoolmaster who watched by the bedside while all
the others were in church thought that he was about to die.
Hardly had the Mass finished, however, than he spoke.

"My friend," he said, " a great change has taken place. I'm
cured."

Indeed his strength came back to him very quickly and by 20
May he was able to offer Mass, though as he was still unable to
fast for long he said it at two in the morning. Needless to say that
the church was full. Dr Saunier still forbade him to do any work,
and as he hobbled into church every day on the arm of the schoolmaster all that he could do was to cast longing eyes on the confessional.

It was known that Abbé Vianney had desired to live a little
longer in order to prepare himself properly for death. As the weeks
went by and he husbanded his strength, anxiety grew in the parish.
On all sides it was believed that he was preparing to leave them for
the solitude that he earnestly desired. After a few weeks he was
allowed back into the confessional, and he began once more his
daily programme, beginning at one in the morning despite the pro-
tests of his friends. On one thing, however, the doctor insisted:
until he was completely recovered he was to take two meals a day,
eat a little meat at midday and drink a little wine—a quarter of a
glass of old Bordeaux—at each meal.

He looked old beyond his years and a visiting priest considered that he would not last more than a month or two. The bishop
and the doctors urged him to take a holiday away from the crowds
of pilgrims. Abbé Raymond, he was told, could look after the
parish in the meantime. Abbé Vianney considered the matter and
the more he did so the clearer it became to him that here was the
chance that he needed; he could go on holiday to his brother's

farm at Dardilly; once there, need he return to Ars? He wrote off
to the bishop, asking to be given the chapel of the Minims at
Montmerle where the only duty was the morning Mass, and
prepared to leave the parish.

He had endeavoured to keep his plan secret but news leaked out
and on 11 September, the night fixed for his departure, parishioners were stationed at strategic points in the village to prevent
his going. At one o'clock in the morning (12 September) he was
seen to leave the presbytery carrying a small parcel with his
breviary under his arm. He eluded the watchers and made off over
the bridge across the Fontblin. Pertinand, the schoolmaster,
managed to catch him up and remonstrate, but to no purpose.
The pair of them continued the journey together.

At Ars Abbé Raymond was in his element. The pilgrimage
would be organized as it should be. Yet even now he seems to have
been unaware of the true state of affairs, though it was very soon
brought home to him. Without Abbé Vianney there was no
pilgrimage, or at least there was none at Ars; it had been transferred to Dardilly. Directly it was known that Abbé Vianney was
with his brother, parishioners from Ars began to make the journey there; news of his arrival in the village near Lyon caused
pilgrims to come from that city. Finally Abbé Raymond was
obliged to recognize that without its parish priest Ars was little
different from any other parish. He began to take steps to secure
Abbé Vianney's return, seeking out the bishop and journeying to
Dardilly with a letter from him, the long-awaited answer about
the chapel at Montmerle. Abbé Vianney tore it open: Montmerle, he learned, was out of the question, but the bishop was
able to offer him the chaplaincy at Beaumont, though he urged
on him reflexion, ought he not perhaps to stay in Ars after
all?

He decided that he would travel to Beaumont, say Mass there
and make up his mind, for in spite of his great desire for solitude
he was in a state of indecision. His brother, on the other hand, was
not sorry to see him go; the life of the farm had been upset by the
callers who came at all hours.

"I am no longer master in my own house!" he exclaimed.

Once more Abbé Vianney set off long before dawn, encountered Abbé Raymond at Albigny, said Mass, and continued the journey to Beaumont. At Saint-Merle, directly it was known that the Curé d'Ars had entered the village, people flocked to the church. Despite his fatigue he was obliged to preach to them, and then a carriage was found and the two priests continued their journey to Marlieux where they spent the night at the presbytery. Next morning both said Mass at Beaumont. As they left the chapel Abbé Vianney told Abbé Raymond his decision.

"God does not want me here," he said.

"Where will you go then?"

"We must return to Ars."

They set off together in a carriage. At Ambérieux Abbé Vianney decided to walk.

"The carriage tires me," he said, "I'll complete the journey on foot."

At Savigneux, while he rested a little, a messenger was despatched to Ars so that as the two priests entered the village they did so to the sound of the church bells ringing a merry peal. At about five in the afternoon, as Abbé Vianney, leaning on a stick, made his way down the village street, the parish turned out in force to meet him. To the rousing welcome that he received he could hardly reply. Emotion overcame him.

"I'll never leave you again," he muttered, "I'll never leave you again."

On Abbé Raymond's arm he walked round the square in front of the church, blessing his parishioners, and then set off for the *Providence* to see the children. He was dropping with fatigue but went into the church for night prayers, which were said a little earlier so that he could go to rest. For the next few days he was able to enjoy a little quiet as the pilgrims had ceased coming during his absence, but they soon found him out again, and it was not long before his days resumed their usual pattern.

*   *   *

Two events with which Abbé Raymond was concerned require some mention at this point. They are the transference of the direction of the *Providence* to nuns and the incident of La Salette. With the first his intervention was slight; he merely concurred with episcopal directions, though on a final analysis the changes at the *Providence* went very much against the wishes of its founder. With the second it is not going beyond the facts to say that he was to some extent the cause of the difficulties provoked by Abbé Vianney's change of mind regarding the authenticity of the children's visions which were alleged to have taken place in 1846.

Abbé Vianney's serious illness and his attempted escape from the burden of the parish in 1843 had caused some discussion about the future of the *Providence*. He was its founder and its heart and soul. He provided for it, begged for it, was its inspiration. As one biographer puts it, he *was* the *Providence*. What he did not understand was that, although he had provided for its future by training young women to run it, he could not guarantee that his successor in the parish would be a man of his calibre, able to do what he had done. In order to assure its continuance on a firm foundation it was suggested that it should be placed under the direction of nuns. In addition to this advantage it was urged that with nuns the place would be cleaner and better run, the children would be better taught.

All this was true but it entailed changing the character of the work. It is a common enough phenomenon with religious institutions. After the first flush of early enthusiasm there comes the period when the work either develops to a degree that had not been foreseen or else settles down to a placid, uninspired existence and gradually peters out. In order to prevent the latter eventuality it was proposed to hand over the *Providence* to nuns, though by doing so it meant making it an institution, endowing it with a respectability which would effectively rob it of some of its own particular spirit. As it had begun it was a family affair, existing from hand to mouth, dependent on the inspiration and drive of the priest who had founded it. At all events Abbé Vianney was opposed to this transformation of his work. He looked forward to the time when he could retire there and be left in peace; the women in charge, whom he knew well, who knew him well, were completely in his confidence, and though he respected nuns, reverenced the vocation and on occasion encouraged women to enter convents, he did not see the *Providence* under their charge.

Abbé Raymond saw the matter differently. "I was among those," he declared, "who urged him to call in the nuns." The bishop shared Abbé Raymond's view and sent an investigator, Canon Perrodin, to talk to Abbé Vianney about the future. (Canon Perrodin, it is interesting to know, had founded a similar house at Bourg which he had entrusted to the Sisters of St Joseph.) The result of their interview was that Abbé Vianney gave way.

An attempt was made to assure the future of the three women who had been running the establishment by sending them off to the mother-house of the nuns at Bourg as novices. But they did not long remain. Catherine Lassagne and Marie Filliat took up residence in rooms near the presbytery where they occupied themselves in mending the church linen and vestments, seeing to the adornment of the church and preparing their parish priest's meals. They also visited the sick.

One of the first steps taken by the nuns was the closure of the orphanage in order to leave them free to concentrate on the school with which they meant to combine a small boarding establishment. Abbé Vianney naturally suffered at this reversal of his whole policy; he had come to regard "his orphans" with especial affection and relied on their prayers. "The *Providence* has been blamed for many things," he remarked to a friend, "and according to some the children were not well behaved, yet God worked miracles for it!" Nevertheless, he accepted the change and after a short interval began once again to go every day to see the children at midday, though to the end of his days he regretted the departure of the orphans.

The change at the *Providence* took place in 1847. In 1849 Abbé Vianney was able to introduce teaching brothers into the parish; they founded a school, and one of them, Frère Athanase, acted as secretary, ran the parish choir, and generally helped with the arrangements of the pilgrimage. For the next ten years he was constantly in Abbé Vianney's company and so became a valuable source of information about this part of his life, a period at which the pilgrimage was at its height.

*   *   *

What has been called the "incident of La Salette" began in 1850 with the arrival in the village of one of the visionaries, Maximin Giraud. The story of the events to which this incident refers goes back to 1846, though despite the fact that devotion to our Lady of Salette has thus been in existence for upwards of a century it has always remained relatively speaking a local manifestation, and since the details of its origin are therefore not well known to English readers it will be well to recapitulate them shortly.

On 19 September 1846, two children, Mélanie Calvat, a girl of fifteen, and Maximin Giraud, a boy of eleven, were minding cattle on a high mountain near La Salette-Fallavaux, not far from Corps, in the diocese of Grenoble.   At about three in the afternoon, according to the children, in the bright sunlight they saw a tall "beautiful lady" (*une belle dame*) curiously dressed and surrounded by a very bright light. She spoke to them partly in French and partly in the local Dauphinois dialect, and as she spoke she was weeping. The principal part of her message was as follows:

"If my people will not submit, I shall be compelled to let go the arm of my Son. It is so heavy and so powerful that I can no longer sustain it. For how long have I suffered on your behalf! If I do not want my Son to abandon you, I must pray to him ceaselessly, though you take no account of it. . . . I have given you six days to work. I have reserved the seventh for myself and yet you do not wish to let me have it. It is this which weighs down so much the arm of my Son. The carters never swear without using the name of my son. These are the two things which are weighing down the arm of my Son. If the harvest is spoilt, it is only because of you. Last year, I showed you this in the potato crop, but you took no notice. On the contrary, when you saw the spoilt potatoes you swore, using the name of my son. The potatoes will go on rotting and, by Christmas this year, there will be none." [1]

The "beautiful lady" then told each of the children a secret, which the other did not hear, and asked them if they said their prayers properly. "Hardly at all", they replied. She told them that they should say at least the Lord's prayer and Hail Mary night and morning and reverted to the impiety of the people, reminding Maximin of the diseased wheat once shown him by his father. Finally she urged on them that they must make all this known to "my people" and disappeared.

The children did so at once and the resultant controversy can be imagined, but through thick and thin, long interrogations and the fierce opposition of some churchmen, they stuck to their story. People began to make pilgrimages to La Salette and miracles were reported. In 1851 the Bishop of Grenoble declared officially that the vision bore the marks of truth, the shrine was built with its church and attendant buildings and our Lady of La Salette took its place as one of the pilgrimage centres of France.

The question of the authenticity of the vision hardly arises in this context, though it will have struck readers that parts of the "message" are couched in strange terms. We are at liberty to receive or reject it, but all that is relevant in the context of Abbé Vianney's biography is his attitude to the affair. Nor need we concern ourselves with the subsequent career of the two children save to remark that it was not very satisfactory. Mélanie's particularly, and that nothing can be proved from this fact. Abbé Vianney saw Maximin in 1850, the year before the episcopal approval mentioned above. Until this interview he had always believed in the vision. What made him change his mind?

Maximin Giraud arrived in Ars on 24 September 1850, towards the end of the day, accompanied by his sister Angélique Giraud, and three men, MM. de Brayer, Verrier and Thibaut. The three latter were supporters of the Baron de Richemont, who was

[1] I have taken this translation of the main part of the message from *The Sun Her Mantle*, by John Beevers (Dublin, 1953), which on pp. 23–109 gives a very clear account of the vision and its history. A more exhaustive treatment may be found in *La grâce de la Salette*, by J. Jaouen, M.S. (Paris, 1946). Both these books conclude that the vision was authentic.

claiming to be Louis XVII, and they hoped to use Maximin in support of their cause. Failing to prevail upon him to admit that his secret referred to the baron they took him off to Ars with the hope that Abbé Vianney would succeed, where they had failed, in extracting the secret.

They were met on arrival in Ars by Abbé Raymond, who, since Abbé Vianney was still in the confessional, took them off to the *Providence*. Abbé Raymond had met Maximin the previous year at La Salette and he remembered that he had been unable to obtain any information from him about the visions; thus it was without any particular prejudice in his favour that he began to question the youth about the purpose of the visit to Ars. He was told that the party had come to consult Abbé Vianney about Maximin's vocation. Abbé Raymond, who did not believe that the boy had seen the vision of our Lady, could not restrain himself from exclaiming that surely one who had seen the blessed Virgin and been entrusted with a secret by her had no need to ask advice about his vocation. And he launched into a diatribe against La Salette, declaiming against false miracles and false witnesses.

"If you dare to claim that you have seen the blessed Virgin, you are a liar . . . !" he exclaimed.

That final remark goaded Maximin into a reply that, from one point of view, was the cause of all the trouble.

"I never said that I saw the blessed Virgin," replied the boy. "All I said was that I saw a beautiful lady. But you can say that I'm a liar if you like. I don't care."

"You only saw a beautiful lady! And I've seen more beautiful ones still. So you see?"

Abbé Raymond went off, remarking as he left the room, "La Salette must be smashed. The child has retracted."

It seems certain that before next morning he had informed Abbé Vianney that Maximin was a liar and had never seen the vision. When therefore the latter had his interview the first words he heard were not calculated to put him in the best of tempers.

"So you're the child who has seen the blessed Virgin?" remarked Abbé Vianney.

The interview lasted for about ten minutes. Maximin saw Abbé Vianney again for a minute at about eleven o'clock and the party left for Lyon by the afternoon coach. After that day Abbé Vianney ceased to believe in the vision of La Salette. To Abbé Raymond he declared, "If Maximin told me the truth he saw nothing . . . he has not seen the blessed Virgin."

There is more than one account originating with Maximin about what passed at the interview. He denied that he told Abbé Vianney that he had not seen the blessed Virgin. He did not make his confession to him, but when tackled with having told lies said that he had lied to the parish priest at Corps (he meant about other, small matters in the past, not the vision). Abbé Vianney, according to Maximin's showing, understood him to refer to the vision, and the boy found the priest hard to understand because owing to the very few teeth in his head he seemed to mumble. At all events, on returning to Grenoble he was questioned about what had occurred at Ars and the bishop drew up and dispatched to Abbé Vianney a declaration by Maximin which asserted that he had not denied his vision, had retracted nothing and still stood by his original affirmation that he had seen the vision. The declaration concluded: "If I have made any revelation to the Curé of Ars or told him any secret which prevents him from believing in the apparition of La Salette I readily authorize him to disclose it to the bishop's representatives." Two priests of the diocese of Grenoble took this to Ars, but Abbé Vianney was not to be shaken. Maximin wrote again, insisting that he had been misunderstood. This was sent on by the Bishop of Grenoble, who asked if there had not been a misunderstanding. Abbé Vianney replied:

"I put great trust in our Lady of La Salette; I blessed and distributed many medals and pictures representing the occurrence and I gave away fragments of the stone on which the blessed Virgin sat and always carried one of these fragments with me. I even put one in a reliquary. Few of the priests in your diocese I should think, Monseigneur, have done as much for La Salette as I. I need not repeat . . . what I said to your priests. When the boy told me that he had not seen the blessed Virgin I was exhausted for a couple of days. But after all, Monseigneur, the wound is not very serious and if this occurrence [La Salette] is the work of God it will not be destroyed by men . . ."

There is other evidence of Abbé Vianney's change of mind regarding La Salette after Maximin's visit, and there is evidence also that Maximin, who had heard that at Ars consciences were read, decided to put the matter to the test by telling a pack of lies. At all events for eight years Abbé Vianney refrained from propagating devotion to our Lady of Salette. At the very end of his life he appears to have recovered belief in the vision, to some extent at least. Abbé Raymond, who had partly provoked the whole incident, did not let it rest there but wrote off to the Archbishop of Lyon, Cardinal de Bonald, an account of the affair. This letter may well have prompted the Cardinal to endeavour to discover the secrets entrusted to the two children. The negotiations which resulted finally in their being communicated, not to him but to Pius IX, are outside the scope of this book.

The authenticity of the vision of La Salette was canonically approved by the Bishop of Grenoble in 1851; even this did not cause Abbé Vianney to change his mind. The two books that have been quoted as the authority for some of the statements in this chapter, as well as others both on the question of La Salette and on the life of Abbé Vianney, ascribe his change of opinion after the interview with Maximin to a misunderstanding occasioned by Abbé Raymond's first report to him and the conduct of the boy when he saw him. It seems strange that the priest, who for many years gave evidence of extraordinary intuition both in the confessional and out of it, should have failed so signally in connexion with La Salette. His questioning of the boy should have shown him clearly, from ordinary human experience, the type of person with whom he was dealing. His impression of what was said to him was evidently very clear indeed, since despite the later written declaration, sent on to him with episcopal authority, he persisted in his attitude. If we must choose between Abbé Vianney and Maximin it seems obvious whose account should be preferred.

When some years later he appeared to change his mind again and revert to his former belief in the authority of the visions, there is no denying that his attitude is not the enthusiastic one displayed before he made contact with Maximin. He seems to have scrupled to persist in his denial after the Bishop of Grenoble's approval, though it should hardly need pointing out that Abbé Vianney, and anyone else, was at perfect liberty to hold the opinion that the diocesan commission had come to the wrong conclusion. The fact of the visions and the message of La Salette are not an article of faith, and if he doubted them Abbé Vianney could plead that he was in good company for his attitude was shared by more than one eminent churchman.

His refusal, persisted in for some years in the face of the findings of the Bishop of Grenoble's canonical commission, was not due to Abbé Raymond's influence; it was certainly not strong enough to have imposed so striking a change of attitude which was founded in fact on the interview with Maximin. That is clear. It is also clear that Abbé Raymond was a great trial to Abbé Vianney during all the years that he acted as his curate. We have seen that he hoped to succeed to the parish and on more than one occasion he acted as if he believed himself already possessed of that office. Catherine Lassagne declared that "he was sent by God to exercise the patience of his good servant", and the mayor of Ars considered that though appointed assistant in the parish he acted as Abbé Vianney's tutor.

When he arrived in the parish he was lodged at the presbytery and there installed himself in the room until then occupied by Abbé Vianney, leaving the latter a damp and dark room on the ground floor. The parishioners protested and Abbé Raymond found lodgings in the village. He had been appointed assistant priest, but at once began to behave as if he were in charge. He treated Abbé Vianney harshly, without regard for his age and holiness, and, as may be expected, tactlessly. He signed his name in the parish register after a baptism, *Raymond, Curé*, and if that rings a little ambiguously—after all he had been a parish priest before coming to Ars—on another occasion he subscribes *Raymond, Curé de ladite pariosse*—'parish priest of the aforesaid parish'. He contradicted Abbé Vianney in the pulpit and was known to have remonstrated with him for not telling him everything or for not running the pilgrimage as he thought it should be run, yet Abbé

Vianney defended him before the people of Ars, and when the bishop sent Abbé Dubuois to find out the true position, exclaimed, "Oh, leave him here with me; he tells me home-truths!" After Abbé Raymond's departure Abbé Vianney told another priest that he did not correct him sufficiently: "I am not as well off as before." He wrote to the bishop on one occasion, concluding his letter: "I have nothing special to say to your Lordship about M. Raymond save that he deserves a special place in your heart as a reward for all his kindness to me. . . ."

Although Abbé Vianney suffered it all humbly and patiently enough, others were not so heroic as he and could not bear to see him treated high-handedly. It was intimated to him that the state of affairs had gone on long enough. He wrote, or rather dictated, the terms of a letter to be written to the bishop asking for the curate's removal, but when it was brought for signature tore it up. This occurred in Holy Week. "I have thought about it," he explained. "Our Lord bore his cross during these hallowed days; I must do the same." Not long afterwards the mayor went to see the bishop, intending to say something of the curate, but found that he was forestalled by a letter from Abbé Vianney asking that "his beloved M. Raymond" be left with him a little longer. Finally, the general feeling penetrated even Abbé Raymond's thick skin and he asked to be moved. "You have been so useful to me," wrote Abbé Vianney after his departure, "you have done so much for me, that you have captivated my heart." Abbé Raymond came to appreciate his former parish priest and went to see him shortly before his death. He gave evidence for the process of canonization and remarked that his only regret was not to have profited sufficiently by the example that he had before his eyes. "I count, nevertheless," he concluded, "on the kind and paternal affection which he showed me."

Both men, it seems, profited by their eight years together. It is an apt illustration of a remark of the late Abbot Cuthbert Butler's when speaking about the prayer of acts of the will. "When privileged to give the retreat to the secular clergy," he writes, "I have suggested this act of resignation as one sometimes likely to be suitable for parish priests: 'O my God, for love of thee, and in conformity to thy holy will, I resign myself to put up with this uncongenial curate for as long as the bishop shall leave him with me.' Not only is this a very real act of conformity to God's will in something trying, and so of the very highest order of virtue and love of God; but if the curate also prays likewise, *mutatis mutandis*, it is certain that, both having prayed like this for their half hour of mental prayer, their mutual relations are likely to be greatly eased and improved."[1] Abbé Vianney certainly showed a high degree of virtue in bearing with Abbé Raymond. His next curate, Abbé Toccanier, was a more fortunate choice; unlike Abbé Raymond, he later became Curé d'Ars, the second to bear the title that the first had made a household word.

[1] *Ways of Christian Life*, by Dom Cuthbert Butler, Monk of Downside Abbey (London, 1932), p. 222.

CHAPTER XI

THE TEMPTATION TO SOLITUDE

RUNNING through the last quarter-century or more of Abbé Vianney's life is the constantly recurring theme of his desire to leave his parish. Continually he was asking his bishop to allow him to resign and go off to a monastery or some solitary spot, and always he asked in vain. In view of the nature of the life he led at Ars from 1827 onwards this desire for a solitary life can well be understood, yet fundamentally he regarded it as a temptation.

"Monsieur le Curé," asked a priest on one occasion, "how can you resist the temptation to vainglory amid this crowd of people who come here in order to see you, and you alone?"

"Ask me rather," came the answer, "how I continue to resist the temptation to fear, discouragement and despair."

It was fear for his own salvation, the fear of dying with the heavy load of a parish priest's responsibility upon him, that weighed him down. "You don't know what it means to go straight from a parish before the judgement seat of God," he said once to a priest. He regarded himself as ignorant and incapable, Catherine Lassagne tells us; by accepting the post of parish priest he was afraid that he had tempted heaven. That thought was with him until his dying day.

He wanted "a little corner" where he could "weep over his poor life". In 1827 he asked his bishop to allow him to give up his parish, only to be offered another one. Hardly ever did he write to the episcopal curia on business of one sort or another than he added a paragraph or two at the end imploring the same thing. In 1851 Mgr Devie, in order to prepare for his own retirement, obtained a coadjutor. Abbé Vianney took this as a golden opportunity to urge his own case:

"Monseigneur," he wrote, "since you are so fortunate as to see about your own retirement in order to think of nothing save heaven, I implore you to obtain for me the same happiness. If you

leave without granting me this favour I shall die of a broken heart.
... I have every hope that your Lordship will grant me the favour
that I ask . . .—Jean-Marie Vianney, poor Curé d'Ars."

When the coadjutor succeeded to the see, Abbé Vianney
returned to the attack:

"I am becoming increasingly infirm. I am obliged to pass a part
of the night sitting in a chair or to get up three or four times in an
hour. I am subject to fits of giddiness in the confessional where for
two or three minutes at a time I am in a maze. In view of my infirmities I desire to say farewell to Ars for ever.—Vianney, poor
unhappy priest (*pauvre malheureux prêtre*)."

In spite of this he remained at Ars. The bishop was there from
time to time, more frequently perhaps than in other parishes, and
before each visit Abbé Vianney undertook some special penance
and redoubled his prayers, in order to move heaven to help him
with the bishop. At some periods of his life this desire for solitude
appears to have amounted almost to an obsession.

"When I am unable to sleep," he told Frère Athanase, "my
soul goes on a journey. I visit a Trappist or a Carthusian monastery;
I seek a corner to weep over my poor life and do penance for my
sins."

All his prayers appeared to be answered except those which
he made on his own behalf; he once remarked as much to
Catherine Lassagne, only to receive the answer that what he asked
was not in accordance with God's will. To this he had no reply.
In his calmer moments he recognized that his desire for solitude
was a temptation that he had to resist. As we have seen, he generally managed to do so successfully, but at least three times he
was so far carried away as to take the law into his own hands and
endeavour to slip away unperceived.

One night in 1840 he left the presbytery and started off on the
road to Villefranche, but had reached no further than the wayside
cross near Ars when he was overcome by doubts about what he
was doing. He was struck by the thought that possibly the conversion of one soul was worth all the prayers that he could offer in
solitude. He turned back to Ars and it was only some years later
that he revealed the incident.

In 1843, convalescent after his illness, he thought that the time had come when he could at last retire; we have seen how his plans turned out. In 1848 a Capuchin of Lyon received him as a Franciscan tertiary. He asked to join as a friar, but it was explained to him that he would do more good by remaining parish priest of Ars. There was some alarm in the parish at the time—the villagers remembered very vividly the events of 1843—but all became quiet again when it was seen that the Capuchins were not out to capture a valuable recruit for their community.

In July 1852, at the death of Mgr Devie and his succession by the coadjutor, Mgr Chalandon, Abbé Vianney imagined no obstacle remained in the way of his departure. Mgr Devie had always said that he would never allow him to leave the diocese, but now with a new bishop he felt that he stood a better chance. In addition, there had lately been opened at La Neylière, at no great distance away, a contemplative establishment of Marists whose founder, Abbé Colin, he remembered from seminary days. In fact everything seemed to combine to favour his project of retirement. After Abbé Raymond's departure from the parish in 1853 Abbé Toccanier was appointed curate; he was a very different character from his predecessor, and the fact that he belonged to a community of diocesan missioners held the advantage that further assistance could be procured from the same quarter if need be.

Even before Abbé Toccanier's arrival in the parish Abbé Vianney's plans were made. He confided in Catherine Lassagne that this time he really was leaving, but vowed her to secrecy. After the installation of Abbé Toccanier on the morning of Sunday, 4 September, by the vicar-general, Abbé Vianney decided to leave that night; no doubt it was this determination that caused the vicar-general to notice that he appeared a little thoughtful.

Catherine Lassagne found the secret too heavy to bear alone and obtained permission to disclose it to her companion, Marie Filliat. The two women thereupon besought him with tears not to leave the parish. It was in vain. In the circumstances they felt justified in telling the curate, who in turn told two of the teaching brothers. The consequence was that soon after midnight when Abbé Vianney opened his door to slip out he found a small party awaiting him. Events now degenerated into something very like a farce.

"Where are you going?" demanded Frère Athanase. "You want to leave us? Very well I shall sound the alarm bell!"

"Sound it!" replied Abbé Vianney.

Frère Jerome took the lantern and making as if to guide his steps led him towards the road to Villefranche instead of down to the bridge over the Fontblin, intending thus to bring him back by a circuitous route to the presbytery. The ruse failed. Abbé Vianney made off down the road towards the bridge, the little procession of Catherine Lassagne, Marie Filliat, Abbé Toccanier and Frère Athanase bringing up the rear. But the curate perceived that once over the bridge there would be little hope of holding the fugitive. He stepped out in front and barred the way.

"Let me pass!" cried Abbé Vianney. "Let me pass!"

Abbé Toccanier began to reason with him, but finding words entirely without effect stretched forward and snatched the breviary from under his arm.

After vainly demanding its return Abbé Vianney announced that he would say his office on arrival at Lyon.

"What, let a great part of the day pass without saying the Hours," exclaimed one of the bystanders. "What a bad example!"

There was a pause. Evidently the remark had told.

"All right," said Abbé Vianney, "I've another breviary in my room. I shall go back and fetch it."

So the procession returned to the presbytery. On arrival there Frère Athanase ran to the church and rang the bell as if for a fire.

"Monsieur le Curé," they said as the first stroke rang out, "it's the Angelus."

He knelt down and said it with great attention. The curate then proposed that all present should say a decade or two of the rosary for the Curé's safe journey, but his trick was perceived. In order to gain time he hurried to the bookshelf and started to mix up the volumes of the breviary. It was the large octavo, eight-volume breviary bequeathed to Abbé Vianney by Mgr Devie. As the appropriate volume was being sought Toccanier's eye lighted on the bishop's portrait gazing down disapprovingly on the strange scene.

"Look, Monsieur le Curé," he exclaimed. "See how from heaven Monseigneur looks down on you with reproach in his eyes. You respected his wishes when he was alive—you should do so now he is dead. Remember what he told you ten years ago."

"He will not reprove me," came the answer. "He well understands my great need to go away and weep over my poor life."

Picking up the large breviary he made for the staircase, only to run straight into the mayor. The ringing of the bell had roused the village. Fearing fire, robbers or invasion the peasants came flocking with any weapon on which they could lay their hands. Effectively they barred Abbé Vianney's passage and he stood there like a beast at bay. To the villagers were joined the women pilgrims whose turn it was for confession, all crying out that he was not to leave them before finishing what he had begun. The mayor, seeing that he wavered, asked him to come to the sacristy where he had something to tell him. Abbé Vianney agreed. Once in church he fell on his knees and prayed for some time, then rising followed the mayor to the sacristy; before the latter could begin his remonstrances Abbé Vianney flung on his surplice and stole and scuttled off to his confessional.

So the episode, which reads like a strange frustration dream from an analyst's notebook, came to an end. It was the last time that Abbé Vianney attempted to run away; had he reached Lyon it is probable that there would have been considerable difficulty in effecting his return for arrangements had been made for his transport from there to La Neylière, and once he had begun a monastic life it seems unlikely that he would easily have abandoned it. A little later he endeavoured indeed to go to the death-bed of his brother François, but he set off publicly, by carriage, in the company of Abbé Toccanier, who was there to make sure that he returned. When the journey had to be abandoned on account of the heavy snow there was nevertheless great relief in Ars.

Two other odd episodes in the latter part of Abbé Vianney's life require mention at this point. It is not untrue to say that in the

fifties of last century he was the best-known priest in France and
the crowds that flocked to Ars on their return home spread his fame
far and wide. Yet he had received no public recognition of the
fact, no title of honour. He was neither Monseigneur Vianney nor
even Canon Vianney, but plain Abbé or Monsieur Vianney. And
so he desired to remain.

On becoming bishop of Belley Mgr Chalandon decided to
alter this state of affairs. He would turn M. l'Abbé Vianney into
M. le Chanoine Vianney. In company with his vicar-general and
the Mayor of Ars he presented himself at the church door. Abbé
Raymond, who was just reaching the end of his period as assistant
and was in the secret, awaited them; directly they appeared he
sent off a message to Abbé Vianney, who was in the confessional.
The latter, catching up the holy water vessel and sprinkler on his
way, hurried off to the church door to do the proper liturgical
honours, and, since it was the first visit of his Lordship, considered
it his duty to say a few words of welcome. As he concluded, the
bishop produced from beneath his rochet a canon's cape. As the
black and red silk glinted in the autumn sunlight with the ermine
trimming contrasting with the colours, understanding dawned on
Abbé Vianney.

"No, no, Monseigneur," he protested. "Give it to my good
curate here. It would suit him far better."

The bishop took no notice. With the help of the vicar-general
and the curate the cape was forcibly put on the unwilling canon
and as he tried to divest himself of it the bishop managed to do up
the buttons.

"Truly, Monseigneur . . ." began Abbé Vianney, still struggling
to pull it over his head.

The bishop cut short the discussion.

"*Veni Creator Spiritus*," he intoned.

All present fell on their knees for the first verse. As the hymn
continued the strange procession formed up. The bishop and his
assistants, together with Abbé Vianney, half in, half out of the
cape, entered the church and made their way through the crowds
up the aisle and into the sanctuary. Abbé Vianney hurried off to
the sacristy to rid himself of the offending garment. When

the mayor told him that to do so would be to insult the
bishop he desisted and stood there, a dejected shame-faced figure,
as the bishop sang the collect and then addressed the congregation.
Afterwards, looking like a condemned criminal, he went back to
the presbytery with the bishop, but no sooner had the latter left
than Abbé Vianney was offering his canon's cape for sale round the
village. In the end he sold it for fifty francs (two pounds) to a
parishioner and wrote to the bishop to inform him of what he had
done:

"Monseigneur, the cape that you bestowed on me has given
me great pleasure. As I was unable to complete a foundation [of a
mission] I sold it for fifty francs. And I was very glad to obtain
this price for it."

So much for the ecclesiastical authorities. The civil government
was no more fortunate. The *sous-préfet* of Trévoux (it is not
recorded whether it was the same who, many years previously,
had been reproved for the dances and soirées at his residence) sent
off a report to the *préfet* about Ars and its parish priest.

After relating the enhanced position of this little village,
"formerly the most unknown in this district", he asserted that all
was due to "the holiness of a modest priest whose evangelical faith
is such as to move mountains". And so on. The *préfet* sent on the
report to Paris, and after the usual delay the official circular
announced that "M. le Chanoine Vianney" was gazetted Cheva-
lier of the Imperial Order of the Legion of Honour. It remained
to obtain the recipient's acceptance. When he heard that there was
a chancery fee of twelve francs, he exclaimed in horror:

"What! pay all that when I've refused. I'd do better to feed
twelve poor men with the money."

Abbé Toccanier paid the fee.

In October the *préfet* arrived in Ars with the intention of pin-
ning the decoration on Abbé Vianney's cassock. His compliments
were cut short, he was exhorted to continue giving a good example
to all in his *préfecture*, and with a blessed medal pressed into his
hand was dismissed. Abbé Vianney hurried back to the confessional.

He never wore the decoration in his lifetime; only when they laid him on his coffin were they able to pin it to his breast. Did they remember what he said about such things when it was remarked to him that all the powers of the earth were combining to do him honour?

"What makes me afraid," he remarked, "is that when death comes and I present myself with these trinkets before the throne of God, he will say, 'Be off, you have had your reward'."

CHAPTER XII

SOME PILGRIMS

FOR upwards of a quarter of a century pilgrims travelled to Ars to consult the parish priest, to be cured of their diseases, to settle vocations, to confess their sins. Cardinals, bishops, priests, civil servants, farm labourers, nuns, monks, friars, society men and women, the famous and the insignificant, those who stood in urgent need of help and those who did not require it, jostled each other in the queue for confession and rubbed elbows in the village street. They slept where they could, finding lodgings with the villagers or further afield, ate what was provided and put up with great discomfort, waiting for days for the sake of a few brief minutes with this priest of a small village, a man of little education who, according to all reports, had failed his examinations and only just achieved ordination.

The stories told by the pilgrims have been collected by Abbé Vianney's biographers, and at Ars and in the papers of the canonization process there is a great mass of evidence which shows how far-reaching was the influence of him who was known everywhere as the Curé d'Ars. In reading the principal biographies—Mgr Trochu's, Abbé Monnin's, Joseph Vianney's—one is struck by the fact that in general it is the same stories that are repeated and that the majority of them are of French origin. Of course, the greater number of pilgrims were French, and for obvious reasons, language being one of them, it is to be expected that the emphasis would be on Abbé Vianney's influence on his fellow countrymen. Yet in the second nocturn lessons read at Matins on 9 August the breviary speaks of pilgrims coming not "only from France and Europe but even from distant parts of America". Unfortunately few of the English-speaking pilgrims seem to have left accounts of their visit to Ars, and of those surviving, either in manuscript or in print, not all are worth reproducing. It is likely that there are some others in existence which have not come my way, letters or diaries preserved among family papers, or in convent archives for instance, which contain personal impressions of a visit to Ars, but a fairly extensive search has failed to reveal more than a few.

Of the printed accounts of English authorship by far the most helpful is that by Mgr Ullathorne, the first Bishop of Birmingham. In a letter to be found in his printed correspondence, and in his small book on La Salette, he has left a graphic account of his visit to Ars.

On the 18th of May, 1854, I made a visit in company with a friend to Abbé Vianney. Starting from Lyons, all along the road we met with persons, returning from a similar visit. Ars is like a place of pilgrimage. From Lyons and all the principal towns in the neighbourhood, so great are the numbers of people who visit the Curé, that it has been found necessary to provide daily public vehicles to this church. Conveyances, private as well as public, are frequently met, whilst the poor are seen plodding on foot in the same direction.

We reached Ars a little before eleven, and a good priest, the Curé's assistant, led us by a side door into the church. The first object on which my eyes fell, was the head, face and shrunken figure of the Curé, straight before me, a figure not easily to be forgotten. He was saying his office, and the nave of the church was crowded and heated with the number of people it contained. His face was small, wasted and sallow; many expressive traces were marked around his mouth. His thin hair was white as snow, his expansive forehead pale, smooth and clear, whilst his eyes were remarkably deep in shadow and covered with their lids. He soon moved to a little side tribune in the nave, and holding his breviary in his left hand, and leaning, or rather supporting himself erect, against a pillar of the nave, as if to sustain his feeble frame, he began to preach. As he opened his eyes, they sent forth a light, pale indeed, as if from his incessant fasting, but so preternaturally bright and tranquil, as to awaken at once the deepest interest. As he went on the vigour and vivacity of his spirit, mantling through his thin and suffering frame, increased in energy. His voice, soft, yet shrill, rose into cries of anguish as he spoke of sin, his contracted hand was placed between his eyes, his brows shrank together, and his tears began to fall, as they always do when the thought of sin comes to his mind. He opened again his eyes, and those shaded recesses became full of light; and he threw his feeble hand appealingly towards the people, who, fixed in the positions they had first taken, listened with profound attention, and even awe. Then his eyes were cast up, and his whole figure seemed to follow. He spoke of God, so good, so amiable, so loving, and his hands, his shoulders, his very person, seemed to gather on his heart. It was impossible not to feel that God alone was there, and was drawing the whole man to that seat of his repose. Then there was a word about being in the Heart of Jesus, and in that word one felt that he was *there*. He spoke for twenty minutes, and with a simplicity, a self-abandonment, an energy, and variety of tone and action, as his subject varied, all spontaneous from the heart. One thing I cannot describe—such a force of spirit, with such an absence of animal warmth; it was as if an angel spoke through a body wasted even to death. Owing to the loss of his teeth, and to my distance from him, I could not well make out the words of his discourse, but if I had not understood a syllable, I should have known, I should have felt that one was speaking who lived in God. His instruction was on confession, and was interspersed with one or two brief anecdotes and many ejaculations. He then went out, and in his surplice, bareheaded, for he never covers his head, proceeded through the hot sun to visit a sick person. A crowd followed, and pressed upon him.

Before he reached his house, I had looked over it with his Reverend assistant. The walls were naked and ruinous; there was scarcely anything there besides the poor furniture in his own room and his little bed. In one room, however, as ruinous as the rest, there was a good piece of furniture, containing sets of rich vestments, which the Marquis of Ars, at a cost of 40,000 francs (£1,600), had presented to his church. Before he came in I was told he would escape from me as soon as he could for a little solitude. But no. His manner of receiving me was as free and simple as it was full of humility and charity. There was nothing of a tone and gesture straining itself to maintain a character, but the disengaged self-abandonment and simple politeness of a saint. The chair which he presented was recommended as the chair of his predecessor in the parish. And often he repeated that he was very grateful for my visit. I was speaking of prayer for England, and the sufferings of our poorer Catholics on account of their faith; and he was listening, his eyes nearly closed, when suddenly he opened their singular light in all its brightness full upon me, and breaking in on the narrative in a way I shall never forget, with the manner of one giving a confidence, he said: "But I believe that the Church in England will return to its ancient splendour." . . . To understand him one should see his face, always glowing when he speaks of God, always bursting into fits of tears when he thinks of evil. His poor eyes, though so sweet and tranquil, are worn with his tears and habitually inflamed.

His spirit of direction has that largeness in it which only prayer and a long experience of souls can attain to, unless it be infused. . . . I felt it would be wrong to detain him from his short time for rest and food, so I asked him for a medal by which to remember him. He took a few in his hand and said:

"Take one."

"No," I said, "give me one."

"There," he said, "is the Immaculate Conception; and there is St Philomene."

It is not true that this holy priest has predicted evils on France, as has been related; or that he has a special medal which he blesses for the protection of those who wear it against coming calamities. At my request he saw my companion for a short time, and saying he would go and meet him, he had no sooner shown himself at the door than the crowd of people rushed upon him. He can never stir out without being thus surrounded and pressed on by the people. He took my friend affectionately by the hand, and walked with him round his little garden, and when an offering was made to him for his church, he said, "Oh, let it be for my poor". He was then left to himself, but his meal was quickly over, and he returned to the confessional. He is now required by his bishop under obedience, to add to the one single poor meal, that used to be all he had in the day, a second, and to eat a little meat at one of them. At this he sheds tears—that a sinner like him should eat meat; and he thinks himself a glutton.[1]

[1] *The Holy Mountain of La Salette*: A pilgrimage of the year 1854, by the Right Rev. Bishop Ullathorne (London: 1854), pp. 129–33.

Mgr Ullathorne was greatly impressed by the numbers of pilgrims and by the long periods passed by Abbé Vianney in the confessional:

> He never begins his labours in the confessional later than two o'clock in the morning, often at one, and when the numbers waiting are very great, at midnight. Penitents will lie all night on the grass, fifty at once, either in order to gain the earliest admission to the church and the confessional, or because of the houses being already completely filled with those who come from a distance. Except while he says Mass, or preaches his little discourse, or for the very short time he takes for his scanty food, the holy Curé lives almost entirely in the confessional. From midnight or early morn he is there until nine at night; then he retires for his office, a little reading, and some two hours at the very most for rest. Such has been the unbroken course of his life for many years.[1]

In the letter written to a nun at St Dominic's, Stone, Mgr Ullathorne gives very much the same description of Ars and its parish priest as he does in his short book on La Salette. He adds, however, one or two details, missing from the longer account. Thus, of the remark referring to the future of the Church in England, we are told: "He said [it] with a voice as firm and confident as though making an act of faith. . . I am sure he firmly believes this from whatever source he has derived the impression."

Ullathorne goes on to describe the experience of making his confession to Abbé Vianney:

> I then asked him to hear my confession and manifestation. At each point which tended to a question his words were few, simple, penetrating, but exceedingly large in their charity to the individual to whom they were addressed. With him the Spirit is everything, the form and manner of action of little consideration, so long as God is the object of the soul: the Spirit of God, the protection of the Blessed Virgin. On one practical point he gave a practical decision. It was precise, clear, and

---

[1] *The Holy Mountain of La Salette*, p. 134.

satisfying. He knelt by my side when he had concluded, as he did before he began, and I felt it was a moment of grace.[1]

Later on in his book Ullathorne refers to Abbé Vianney's change of mind with regard to La Salette; he traces the history of the incident, but since his information was all derived from what he heard after he had left Ars some of his facts are either wrongly dated or seen in a wrong perspective. He is at pains to explain away the incident, and quotes, as the final proof, a letter written to him by another hand but signed by Abbé Vianney. Ullathorne writes: "Whilst this chapter was going through the press I received a letter from the Curé d'Ars. It is written by the hand of another person, but it is signed by the holy Curé, and bears date 10 July, 1854. In it he says: 'On the apparition of the Blessed Virgin at La Salette, since his Lordship the Bishop of Grenoble preaches it and the Sovereign Pontiff, it is said, approves of it, I believe that you may speak of it in all surety of conscience.'"

Examination of Abbé Vianney's statement shows that he does not say that he believes in La Salette but that in surety of conscience Mgr Ullathorne may speak of it; this is merely another way of saying that it has ecclesiastical approval; one may believe it, one is not obliged to. Mgr Ullathorne made Ars an incidental reference in his book on La Salette; in the life of Abbé Vianney La Salette is no more than that, an incident, though there is cause for gratitude that it drew from Ullathorne that description of Ars in his characteristic style.

Another English bishop who was connected with Ars, though indirectly, was Mgr Arthur Riddell (1836–1907) who was Bishop of Northampton from 1880 until 1907. His mother, Mrs Widdrington Riddell, of Felton (she was the Hon. Catherine Stapleton, sister of Lord Beaumont), was told by Abbé Vianney when she visited Ars that one of her sons would be a bishop. It only came to the knowledge of her son Arthur when his appointment to the see of Northampton was published, but though prudently concealing the prophecy from her son his mother firmly believed it and there is evidence of this in the pectoral cross which she bought

---

[1] *Letters of Archbishop Ullathorne* (London, 1892).

soon afterwards and before her death bestowed on her eldest son; he never became a bishop but was able to give it to his brother when he was made Bishop of Northampton. This cross is now at Bishop's House, Northampton.

Mgr Ullathorne described Abbé Vianney as he was in 1854; another description, undated, though certainly referring to the last years of the Curé's life, and probably to a later date than Mgr Ullathorne's book, is to be found in a letter from Sister Mary of the Holy Cross (Roskell) written to her cousin, a canoness of New Hall, Mother Aloysia James Kendal. In the course of a detailed account of a visit to Ars the former writes: "The pictures one sees of the dear old saint sometimes are really dreadful, almost caricatures; the Curé was short in stature and very thin and emaciated, a very high forehead and hair long and as white as snow and straight, *not* turned in at each side of the face as often seen in his pictures. As for his eyes it is impossible to describe them, I never saw any like them, they were large and dark and shone as with a light from heaven and when raised seemed to look through you and far beyond. . . ." [1]

All the pilgrims who wrote of Abbé Vianney seem to have been struck by his appearance and by his long hours in the confessional. In 1854, and again in 1855, Canon R. Smith of Penrith made a pilgrimage to Ars on behalf of Mgr Newsham, the then president of Ushaw (he was appointed in 1837 and is regarded as the second founder of the college), who was afflicted with deafness and was concerned, it appears, as to whether he should retire. Canon Smith was to ask Abbé Vianney for a cure and consult him about the president's future course of conduct.

In 1854 Canon Smith reports back: "This morning after seeing the *Vicaire* I received for answer from him that the Curé promises to pray for your cure, and recommends you, once more to recommence a novena, but to my grief I understand that he doubts if it be the will of God you will be cured. As regards the other question he is quite decided, namely, 'go on to the last, just as you are doing'." In a later letter Canon Smith pointed out that it was said

[1] Sister Roskell wrote this letter in her old age as it is dated 18 February 1911 and referred to events that had happened at least fifty-two years beforehand.

that when Abbé Vianney said that someone would be cured it would certainly take place, when he said that a novena was to be made, it was doubtful.

Later in the letter the canon paints a picture of the conditions under which Abbé Vianney lived. It is added testimony to some that has already been quoted in this book but is worth putting down here as the evidence of a north-country parish priest who knew what he was talking about. Can we perhaps detect in the first sentence a wistful note betraying that the canon is speaking from personal experience?

Before saying anything about [another matter] let me remark how much it would edify Professors and students to see the profound respect and devotedness with which the younger clergy treat their senior and superior, the Curé at Ars. Next, that most certainly his life itself is a continual miracle. He has just now at midday [i.e. on Sunday, 9 July 1854] left the church followed by a crowd eager to stop his way to his house, and yet he has been in the church from *midnight* up to now in the confessional all the time except during his mass and office. No one spares him. Everyone seems to insist on seeing him and being heard, no matter what becomes of the Curé meanwhile: he will not hinder anyone—and when he must positively have done, a priest takes him by the hand and leads him away. His last, and I think, first attack is from a good many well-fed looking beggars: his patience seems positively proof against everything. I can see there are some regular bores to manage; for instance one . . . bothering Frenchman insisting on publishing prayer-books, pictures and wonderful things as if in his name and under his sanction, and going perpetually about and after him to appear in his confidence . . .

Canon Smith, like Mgr Ullathorne two months beforehand, raises the matter of prophecies of calamities to come. With the "message" of La Salette still fresh in men's minds it is not surprising that rumours had got about that Abbé Vianney had foretold perils of a similar nature:

"As regards medals, that account of his having had a medal struck turns out to be false: and also that it is certain that he has

not ever foretold any bad times coming, and never speaks of the
present times—refusing to have anything whatever to do with
politics, at least as far as giving opinions to the public."

In September of the following year Canon Smith was back in
Ars on the same mission on behalf of Mgr Newsham. From his
account, written the day after arrival, it emerges that the President
of Ushaw was still worried about whether he should continue in
office, and we are able to discern that there was more at stake than
merely one man's personal problem. The seminary question in
England was also involved, as can be seen from the references to
Cardinal Wiseman.

Ars, Friday, September 21
St Matthew's day, 1855.

REV. AND DEAR SIR.

Thanks be to God this part of my business, by far the most
important of the two, has been settled with complete clearness
and decision. Last night on arriving I went to the younger
priest [Abbé Toccanier], a missioner who seemed to me a most
clear-headed and kind man. I thought it best to explain the case
to him in confidence: to get him to write it down for the
Curé of Ars to think upon through the night—moreover for
him to explain the whole case from the writing to the Curé
and then leave the writing with him. All this was done with
great care on both sides.

I divided the questions into these three: 1° as regards your
holding on and keeping as you are and where you are to end.
2° Your cure. 3° What he had to say as a help to your salvation.
On the first point I explained everything about those very great
difficulties coming from an unjust and natural opposition—
on the second the great advantage of a cure—on the third your
own words . . .

After night prayers the missioners went and consulted with
the Curé; the one I had spoken to came and said, "You must
come at seven tomorrow morning and he will give a decisive
answer to all this." I went to the church at a quarter past four
this morning—the Curé had been hearing confessions since one
o'clock as usual. At seven I was taken into the vestry to him—
he took the greatest interest in me as being sent by you, took my

hand in both his and answered on all the points with the greatest assurance and good will. He said: "Mgr Newsham *is by no means to retire from his present position—his mere presence will be an infinite good*": he repeated those words, "*Sa seule présence sera un bien infini*".

To the second question he answered "*Je ne crois pas qu'il sera guéri*" [I do not think that he will be cured].

About the third he smiled in a sort of humble way and in a somewhat less firm manner said "*que Monseigneur Newsham essaie toujours à tendre vers la perfection*" [Let Mgr Newsham endeavour always to tend to perfection]. But his manner on that point seemed to say "Oh, let him go on". But on all these points he showed a most marked interest in them: quite different from ordinary questions. . . .

To finish off then I said, "*La Sœur Marie de la Croix est en Angleterre—elle est novice dans une maison Carmélite—dans ce temps faut-il la faire soumettre en tout comme Novice, ou faut-il la ménager?*" [Sister Marie de la Croix is in England—she is a novice in a Carmelite convent; during this time is she to be made to undergo everything like a novice, or should she be given special treatment?] He answered immediately twice: "*En tout, comme une novice*" . . . [Everything, like a novice].

One of the missioners who was present at the consultation last night told me four or five words of the Curé which he did not say to me but said to the missioners last night. These words were, "*Et qu'il écoute le Cardinal*". I had previously (last night) told the missioner how true a friendship had ever existed between you and Cardinal Wiseman, but that several bishops wanted to have seminaries of their own regardless of what might result from that to the one great and firmly established seminary. It seems to me then that he has marked out two things, a clear course and authority for guidance . . .

Ever respectfully, Yours
R. SMITH

The Soeur Marie de la Croix mentioned above was Mélanie, one of the visionaries of La Salette, who had gone as a novice to the Carmelite convent at Darlington—this was one of her many abortive attempts to become a nun. After two years there she left, having previously behaved rather oddly, throwing over the wall letters intended for correspondents in France whom she hoped would arrange for her removal from the convent. A letter from Abbé Toccanier, written in October 1855, inquires of Canon Smith whether it is true that Mélanie bears the stigmata, a rumour to that effect being current in France. It seems in fact to have been without foundation. Mélanie died in 1904 in Italy, having previously published what she asserted was her secret in a book full of odd and even fantastic ideas which quickly found its way onto the Index.

Reports of events in Ars in the English press were usually taken from the French newspapers, and on more than one occasion we find *The Tablet* quoting *L'Univers*; in 1859 Abbé Vianney's death is chronicled within about a week of its occurrence. Oddly enough, in the issue of the following week, dated 20 August 1859, referring to Père Lacordaire's candidacy for the French Academy and his work for education, Abbé Vianney is mentioned as still alive and is described as the "celebrated ascetic, the Curé d'Ars, near Lyon, whose reputation for holiness has attracted so many strangers to the humble village of which he is pastor that a line of omnibuses from the Croix Rousse direct to the presbytery he inhabits has been established within the last few years."

Père Lacordaire did in fact visit Ars. After his celebrated conferences in Notre-Dame in Paris and his restoration of the Dominicans in France he was one of the best-known priests in that country. It is certainly true to say that Abbé Vianney was another. Père Lacordaire spent Sunday, 4 May 1845, in Ars. Abbé Vianney was overjoyed to see him, got out the best vestments for his Mass and did everything possible to make him welcome. In the presence of his visitor the Curé preached in the morning at high Mass on the Holy Spirit and made a great impression. Lacordaire sang Vespers the same evening and preached, much to the disappointment of the pilgrims, who had come to hear Abbé Vianney and were not to be satisfied with a substitute, however eminent. The Curé's comment on the day's proceedings was characteristic: "Two extremes met in the pulpit of Ars today," he remarked, "extreme learning and extreme ignorance!"

Founders or would-be founders of religious congregations

journeyed to Ars for advice, bishops came to lay their difficulties before Abbé Vianney. Mgr Dupanloup went there more than once. When he spoke of his great responsibilities Abbé Vianney offered him comfort by saying that there were many bishops in the Church's calendar but very few parish priests. "I have far more reason to fear than you, my Lord," he concluded. Père Muard, the founder of the Benedictines of La Pierre-qui-Vire, Fr Hermann Cohen, the convert from Judaism who founded the Carmelite Priory in Kensington, Mère Eugénie de Smet, foundress of the Helpers of the Holy Souls, all received encouragement from a pilgrimage to Ars and consultation with its Curé.

Those who could not make the journey wrote letters asking for advice or prayers. When at midday Abbé Vianney returned to the presbytery after his long hours in church he found that having escaped from the pilgrims for a few brief moments he was confronted with a heap of correspondence on his table. It was impossible to reply to them all, he had not always time to read them all. Generally the most important received an answer the general lines of which in earlier days had been indicated to Catherine Lassagne or, latterly, to one of the brothers or to Abbé Toccanier. Most of the letters, naturally enough, came from France, and among these the French bishops appear to have been constant in appealing for prayers and help. Their Lordships of Lyon, Aix, Orléans, Autun, Grenoble, Valence, Gap and Evreux, among others, all wrote at one time or another. From Italy, England, Germany, Ireland and North Africa and further afield came letters requesting help in various difficulties, cures, discernment of vocations, but the general effect of the majority of the letters is to present a vivid picture of the misery and unhappiness in the world among the rich and poor, the important and the insignificant. Daily for many hours in the confessional Abbé Vianney was inundated with the woes of humanity, and even during his short break in the middle of the day he was obliged to read them. It is hardly cause for wonder that sometimes he appears to be weighed down under the immense burden imposed upon him, and that more than once he should have been tempted to escape from it all.

CHAPTER XIII

THE MAN AND THE SAINT

WE have come to a point in this story at which it will be useful to pause and consider some of its more startling aspects. So far the plain facts of Abbé Vianney's life have been related and we have seen him against the background of his daily work at Ars: it is the purpose of this chapter to endeavour to observe him at closer range and at the same time to examine some of the more extraordinary phenomena of his life in the light both of his own personality and the present state of knowledge on these matters.

If it was difficult to get close to Abbé Vianney during the latter part of his life when he was besieged during the day and most of the night by the crowds of pilgrims, it is still more difficult nowadays when as a canonized saint he is proposed to the faithful as an object of veneration. The carved statues of the saints are given a niche in churches, and it seems hard to avoid the impression that canonization, as well as declaring the certainty of a man's or woman's holiness, acts also as a metaphorical niche within which they appear in some sort to be fossilized. Their biographies are very often written to a pattern whose sole purpose is edification and while lip service is paid to the truth, it is the edifying anecdote, true or not, which is given preference. Hagiography for popular consumption has inherited from the Middle Ages an idea of literary integrity which is very far from that prevailing today. The medieval biographer was rarely concerned about scrupulous accuracy, particularly in lives of reputed holy people, when his preoccupation was edification: he saw his object clearly as a contribution to the glory of God by the relation of a devout life, and since nothing appeared more likely to him than God's miraculous intervention in the affairs of humanity he would scarcely be worried about verifying his facts or controlling his sources.

With a man who died only a hundred years ago there would

seem to be little possibility of a legend growing as it has done with earlier saints. We are in possession of the testimony given at the process of canonization and of at least one biography, Abbé Monnin's, written by a priest who had been in close contact with Abbé Vianney and could thus vouch for many of the facts that were related.

Nevertheless, something of a legend has grown up concerning some of the phenomena of Abbé Vianney's life, notably in connexion with the alleged prophecies concerning the future of France. During the 1914–18 war it was rumoured that in his lifetime he had foretold a French victory. The story was a pure invention and was founded on predictions which at the time of the Franco-Prussian war were similarly, and incorrectly, attributed to him. In the same way he was supposed to have prophesied that within a century of his death Ars would have reverted to the state in which he found it in 1818. It is possible to find in Catherine Lassagne's *Petit mémoire* a remark that might be thought to lend some support to this latter story but on examination it proves to refer to something quite different.

"It was [in 1845]", she writes, "on the day that M. Vianney announced that he was to have M. Raymond, the parish priest of Savigneux, as his assistant. During his instruction he said: 'Ars is like a big tree. Cut the roots and the tree will fall; or else it is like well-risen dough which then collapses and is reduced to almost nothing.' No one understood what he meant." [1]

He was referring, it appears, not to his parish but to the pilgrimage, and, in view of the assistant's pretensions, his words were to the point, for without Abbé Vianney there was no pilgrimage, as Abbé Raymond discovered when the man whose place he hoped to take went to Dardilly for a short time; the pilgrims followed him there, and Ars, as a place of pilgrimage, was reduced to "almost nothing". As a parish Ars has remained faithful to Abbé Vianney's teaching, and pilgrims still journey there to visit his tomb.

Even during his lifetime he was credited with speaking of future political developments and on one occasion a nervous

[1] Quoted in Trochu, p. 600.

government instructed a police officer to make a special journey from Lyon to discover what exactly Abbé Vianney had said. It was a fruitless errand, because, as the policeman soon found out, Abbé Vianney had said nothing. His predictions were concerned with religious matters and he never troubled about politics; moreover, he appeared to confine himself to individuals, and the one or two instances of predictions of a wider nature seem, on examination, to have been no more than an expression of opinion that, in the circumstances, might have been made by anyone. Thus at the time of Ullathorne's journey to Ars, already mentioned, it will be remembered that Abbé Vianney predicted that the Church in England would return to its former glory. Yet the very form of the remark—"But I believe that the Church in England will return to its former glory"—appears to be almost the echo of hopes that were common in France and further afield in the middle of the nineteenth century. Newman's conversion in 1845, followed by others in succeeding years, seemed to presage a "second spring" which, in 1854, was still being confidently awaited. Abbé Vianney's uncritical acceptance of what was being commonly said and written at that time about the Church in England is almost to be expected.

Mgr Trochu publishes an impressive list of religious congregations and foundations which in their early stages were encouraged by Abbé Vianney. Men and women who felt called to begin some charitable or missionary work, faced with the great difficulties involved, journeyed or wrote to Ars for advice. In many instances Abbé Vianney's encouragement cannot be said to have amounted to a clear prediction, but merely to an assertion that the contemplated work was a good one and that, all things considered, the person in question seemed called to carry it out. In these circumstances, his advice and encouragement, in view of his reputation for holiness, was very valuable; nor is it strange that in many instances they should have been regarded as predictions of success.

There are nevertheless numerous instances of predictions that cannot be reduced to general terms of advice and encouragement, and for which no other term seems possible. They all concerned the affairs of individuals. Sometimes they seemed to be remarks made lightly on the inspiration of the moment, at others they gave every appearance of being solemn warnings. Instances of both kinds of utterance abound and some of them have already been given. Some others fall naturally into place here.

A certain Mlle Moizin, of Bourg, not far from Ars, was determined that she had a vocation for the cloister but was unable to overcome the opposition of her family. She went off to Ars to consult Abbé Vianney and enlist his aid. "Don't worry," was the laconic advice she received, "all your troubles will be over within a year!" By the end of the year she was dead.

M. Faure of Saint-Etienne wanted to become a Jesuit. "No, my friend," Abbé Vianney advised him, "stay where you are. Life is so short." He, too, was dead within a year at the age of twenty-seven.

Another case concerns two girls who went to Ars to satisfy their curiosity. They arrived at the moment of the mid-morning catechism lesson. At the sight of the curious figure standing there in front of the congregation, an old man with long hair who seemed content to confine himself to the simplest of exhortations, one of the girls commented to her companion on the scene.

"What a figure of fun!" she whispered, "it was hardly worth while coming all this way to see that."

"No, it wasn't worth coming all the way to see this figure of fun, was it, Mademoiselle?" interjected the preacher with a smile on his lips. He then continued the instruction. The girl's embarrassment may be imagined.

After the catechism lesson she sought out Abbé Vianney to apologize. He took it all in good part, succeeded in convincing both girls that they should go to confession and to communion the next morning, and then calling aside the companion of her who had made the remark advised her to look after her friend on the way back as a misfortune would overtake her. "Her salvation will not be in danger," he concluded, "as she will have received communion as viaticum in the morning."

After Mass next morning the girls set off home; in the excitement of the journey Abbé Vianney's warning was forgotten, only to be recalled when the girl who had made the unfortunate remark at Ars cried out that she had been bitten by a snake. No help was available, and eventually she expired by the roadside. Having foreseen the danger, remarks Mgr Trochu, Abbé Vianney might well have done something to avert it, adding that possibly it was only foreseen as a vague misfortune and not perceived in its gruesome details. Yet on occasion warning of danger was accompanied by some sort of advice on how to avoid it or ward it off.

There was the case of the servant girl who, just out of an orphanage at the age of nineteen, set off to Lyon to earn her living. On her way there she visited Ars. Hardly had she entered the church during the catechism lesson when Abbé Vianney stopped his instruction and told her that he wanted to see her afterwards. He then went on with the lesson. Afterwards, when she spoke to him, and before she had recounted anything of her circumstances or intentions, he gave her this solemn warning.

"You are on your way to Lyon. Now, my child, a great danger awaits you there. When you are offered a place, think of me and pray to God."

At a domestic agency she was engaged by a man as a general servant with the proviso that his wife should see her first before the affair was finally settled. An appointment was made for that afternoon. On keeping it she found herself outside the house face to face with the man whom she had met that morning. Unaccountably, at that moment she was seized with overpowering fear and taking to her heels made what speed she could in the opposite direction. The man pursued her for some distance, but desisted when the passers-by began to wonder what was happening. Despite her fear the girl remembered the advice received at Ars and prayed as she ran. Afterwards she discovered that she had nearly fallen into the hands of one Dumollard who some five years later was sentenced to death for the murder of several servant-girls. By reason of Abbé Vianney's timely warning this one lived to give evidence at the murderer's trial.

There are several instances of simpler intuitions (and some have been related in a previous chapter) which occurred very frequently at Ars. The calling of some man or woman out of the queue waiting for confession because they had little time or because Abbé Vianney saw that they were needed at home urgently, identification of someone formerly totally unknown; small matters very often, which in isolation might be put down to a "lucky shot", but which, on account of their very frequency, make such an explanation practically impossible.

Yet it requires emphasizing that it was in the confessional rather than out of it that Abbé Vianney displayed these extraordinary powers to the full. Long-forgotten sins were recalled to penitents, men who had not been to confession for years were reminded of the exact time since their last appearance in the confessional—one on being told by Abbé Vianney of the number of years that had elapsed since his last confession was obliged to take a piece of chalk from his pocket and do the sum on the wall of the church—and advice was given which was exactly to the point often about difficulties that had not been mentioned. It was on this more than on anything else that the great reputation, which drew crowds to Ars, was built.

These phenomena bring us face to face with a problem which crops up in the lives of some of the saints and which, until fairly recently, was never seen as a problem at all by those who took the saints seriously. All these wonders were put down to God's miraculous intervention in the lives of his especial servants; he endowed them with these powers for the sake of the mission that he had laid upon them. As an explanation, this has the merit of simplicity, but its inherent difficulties are too great for it to be put forward as the only possibility in view of certain facts which are now well known. In addition to the curious circumstances that some saints who accomplished much good, perhaps even in a wider sphere than Abbé Vianney, and who had, it seems, greater need of powers of this kind than he—St Vincent de Paul, for example—were without them, it has also to be borne in mind that there are numerous examples of men and women who certainly, so far as human judgement in this matter is ever valid, were not saints and yet appear to have possessed similar powers.

In the case of Abbé Vianney there is the additional problem of the *Grappin* whose manifestations we have already encountered. To put these all down to the devil is another example of an explanation which has the merit of simplicity but raises difficulties of a kind similar to those that we have just considered. It is absurd to say, of course, that Abbé Vianney was canonized by the Church because he gave evidence of these extraordinary powers and was visited by the devil. Any properly instructed Catholic could explain that he was a saint, and declared to be such, because of his practice of virtue to a heroic degree, and that the phenomena of his life were not the cause of his canonization. It is a little surprising to read in a modern work devoted to psychical research at the present day, although the book is by a non-Catholic, that Abbé Vianney was canonized because of the phenomena that he experienced:

> Jean Vianney, the Curé of Ars, was a devout French priest of the nineteenth century who, despite a life of exceptional austerity and humility, was for over twenty years plagued by ghostly visitations. There were inexplicable thuds, rappings, clangings, and yells; his bed was shaken and disarranged,—on one occasion even set on fire; his humble furniture was knocked about; his cherished picture of the Annunciation was smeared with excrement. At first the Curé suspected that people were breaking in ... The Curé died in 1859. Three years later began the Bishop's investigation. Depositions were taken from many witnesses. It seemed clear to the pious that the devil, outraged by all this virtue, had been tormenting the Curé. It was only a matter of time before Jean Vianney was ranked among the saints.[1]

The authority to which reference is given for the facts of the case is Mgr Trochu's biography: one wonders how Dr West managed to arrive at his conclusion from this book. Nevertheless, his statement is evidence of a point of view that is common enough among those who are unacquainted with the real criteria of holiness, and it is not uncommon even among Catholics. A very great deal of the controversy about Teresa Neumann, for example, is

[1] *Psychical Research Today*, by D. J. West, M.B., D.P.M. (London, 1954), pp. 11–12.

due to the fact that the popular Catholic press has presented her in a way that seems to assert that, because she bears the stigmata, therefore she must be a saint. Those who hold that the stigmata in her case are nothing more than natural phenomena are thereupon accused of denying her sanctity; however much they protest that they are passing no moral judgement on Teresa Neumann they are charged with besmirching the name of a holy person. As time goes on, however, it is gradually becoming clearer that theories that have been current for many years are no longer satisfactory. Some of Abbé Vianney's biographers still seem to hold that the various physical or psychical phenomena which occur in the lives of the saints and others are due either to the direct intervention of God, who upsets the laws of nature (i.e. they are miraculous), or of the devil, who for his own purposes produces these strange manifestations. This theory, in spite of its simplicity, is unsatisfactory for many reasons, and principally because it leaves unexplained certain important aspects of the matter.

In Abbé Vianney's life we are not concerned with stigmata, and our investigations can be confined to the various manifestations which have been previously recorded in this book: gifts of clairvoyance, the visitations of the *Grappin*, and so on. All the examples that have been quoted rest on documentary evidence (depositions of witnesses taken under oath in view of the canonization) that has been published. It is possible of course that some of the stories have been magnified unconsciously in the telling—some of them, for example, were not taken down until several years after the event—for human memory is by no means infallible, and a treasured recollection of a time long past, though accurate in its principal features as to the main event which occurred (a cure, a conversion), may suffer from unconscious embroidery. Nevertheless, when due allowance is made for all such inaccuracy there remains a large residue of hard fact which is extraordinary enough to merit attention.

The facts of the *Grappin* visitations belong to this category. If they were not the direct work of the devil, a diabolical manifestation intended to hamper the great work that Abbé Vianney was doing in the parish of Ars and further afield, how are they to be explained? In passing, it may be remarked that in this and similar cases where saints have been afflicted with manifestations of the sort that here concern us, what emerges very clearly is their ineffectiveness and their childishness: the shifting of furniture during the night, strange noises or voices, a picture fouled with excrement, even the burning of the bedclothes during the absence of the sleeper, are after all not likely to prevent a man of the calibre of Abbé Vianney from going on with his work. Those who hold that these things are the direct work of the devil assert that God permits him to annoy the saints and others but does not allow him to go too far in his manifestations; they form an additional trial to be borne by those who are living Christian lives to the full.

On the face of it this explanation is unsatisfactory, for it would include all those manifestations which are usually lumped together under the classification of *poltergeist*, but it contains a clue, I believe, in the use of the word "trial", which, as we shall see, is in this context of particular significance. On the other hand, although it is not especially helpful to talk of poltergeists, since to use this word amounts merely to employing another term to describe the phenomenon, nevertheless what is meant by it is very generally understood and it provides an accurate description of the nature of the *Grappin* manifestations at Ars.

In recent years a great deal of research has been done concerning poltergeist phenomena, and several books examining these occurrences, both in England and elsewhere, have appeared in the last half-century.[1]

Before dealing with the *Grappin* at Ars, which I believe to have been a typical manifestation of the poltergeist category, it will be useful to explore the subject a little further.

Instances have been collected from practically all over the world of the moving of furniture, hurling of crockery and other household objects, loud rappings, heavy thumpings, the setting fire to furniture and bedclothes and even houses, the removal of articles from seemingly inaccessible places (a locked and sealed cupboard,

[1] *Ghosts and Poltergeists*, by the late Fr H. Thurston, S.J. (London, 1953), is one of the best collections. It was published posthumously (edited by Fr J. H. Crehan, S.J.) and is made up of a collection of his articles which appeared in *The Month* and elsewhere.

for example[1]), which seemed to have occurred without any visible human agency. There has been more than one case of coffins being moved about in a sealed vault, though here it is possible to postulate some freak operation of the forces of nature—in one case perhaps movement of the ground caused by the rise and fall of subterranean water.[2] The famous case in Barbados which occurred between 1807 and 1820 appears to be very well authenticated; in spite of the sealing and cementing up of the vault, when it was opened the masons had difficulty in getting the slab of the doorway removed, for an immense leaden coffin was resting against it on the inside. It required seven men to lift it and yet it had been moved into this position. (At the closing of the vault white sand had been spread over the floor, but no mark was found in it.) The other coffins to the number of five or six were scattered about. More recently a further report of disturbed coffins similar to the earlier case has come from Barbados and is reported in the *Journal of the Barbados Museum* as occurring in 1945.

Still more enigmatic are the showers of stones which occur inexplicably for a period and just as inexplicably cease. Fr Thurston mentions the case of St Godric's hermitage in the twelfth century; among other phenomena that took place there was a shower of stones beating against the walls. But there are earlier reports than the twelfth century and instances could be quoted in every century down to and including the present one. Fr Thurston mentions "showers of stones which seem to come from space and are only perceptible when quite near"; what is also remarkable, and has been observed in many cases, is that sometimes the stones fall quite gently in a curved trajectory. Sometimes they are hot. Two fairly modern instances, not mentioned by Fr Thurston, may be quoted:

From four o'clock, Thursday afternoon, until half-past eleven, Thursday night, the houses of 56 and 58 Reverdy Road, Bermondsey, were assailed with stones and other missiles coming from an unseen quarter. Two children were injured, every

[1] Thurston, op. cit., pp. 96 *et seq.*
[2] For example, the well-known cases at Gretford, near Stamford, and at Edgware.

window broken, and several articles of furniture were destroyed. Although there was a strong body of policemen scattered in the neighbourhood, they could not trace the direction whence the stones were thrown. (*The Times*, 27 April 1872.)

The stones in this case do not appear to have fallen gently. A similar occurrence is reported (in the *Daily Mail* for 19 August 1920) of showers of stones breaking the windows of a house in Grove Road, London. Forty policemen watched the house from various positions but the stones continued to fall for some time.

Particular care is necessary, of course, where newspaper reports are concerned, but when allowance has been made for the differing standards of evidence in other ages, the unsatisfactory nature of some reports in our own and for trickery and fraud, there yet remains a residue of well-attested cases which are exceedingly baffling.

Since, so far as we know, Abbé Vianney did not suffer from showers of stones it may appear unnecessary to mention them here. They have been included because poltergeist phenomena follow a definite pattern (showers of stones are a commonly recurring form) and one of the most extraordinary features of these manifestations is that they do so. Indeed, to some extent, a pointer to the authenticity of evidence about them is furnished by the similarity of reports from the most diverse sources. A peasant priest at Ars is afflicted by mysterious happenings at night and describes what has happened. We can be fairly certain that in those days and in that place Abbé Vianney had not studied the matter of poltergeists, yet he describes a typical instance as happening to himself. It is rather as if a man unlearned in medical matters described symptoms of an illness from which he had suffered, leading a doctor to conclude that the disease was measles. What happened to Abbé Vianney was a typical poltergeist manifestation which can be compared with the occurrences at Epworth parsonage (the home of the Wesleys) and other well-known instances.

Having described the manifestations as a poltergeist we are really no nearer a solution of the difficulty; the most baffling problem of all is to find an answer to the question, "What is a poltergeist?" Study of the very considerable literature on the subject will furnish an analysis of many cases but no explanation. Mr Harry Price (in *Poltergeist over England*) devotes a chapter to various theories offered in explanation of these phenomena but comes to no conclusion: "We know nothing whatsoever about *why* poltergeists should infest a place, what they are, how to get rid of them, or how to attract them." Nor can we explain the mechanism of their movements, the source of the energy which moves objects, nor where some of the objects come from or where they go when, as frequently, they disappear. Fr Thurston was puzzled by the same question: "I am a firm believer", he writes, "in the reality of poltergeists and in the impossibility of finding any natural explanation of their recorded activities."[1] At an earlier date he had speculated on the possibility of these activities being due to the abnormal psychic powers of the young person (usually a child, generally a girl, in or beginning adolescence) who seems to be a constant in these cases. (For my own part I would add, or a minister of religion, taken in its widest sense: I wonder if the frequency of poltergeist cases occurring in presbyteries, manses, parsonages, nunneries, etc., has ever been investigated. I believe that there is a reason for this, as I shall attempt to show later in this chapter.) Fr Thurston seemed to postulate the existence of a spirit world, of spiritual agencies, not cogniscible directly by our sense perceptions, which are nondescript, that is neither angelic nor diabolic, a childish or irrational type of being. This raises very considerable philosophical and theological difficulties.

Nowadays investigators are paying increasing attention to the psychological aspect of poltergeist cases, to the emotional conflicts and states to be discovered in some of those persons concerned in these manifestations. A few years ago some discussion was caused when Dr John Layard gave it as his opinion that all true poltergeist phenomena are purposeful and "probably caused by conditions of unresolved tension in the psyche of those involuntarily producing them". Under great tension a temporary dissociation of personality may take place; it is a nervous manifestation that is

[1] Op. cit., p. 152.

by no means uncommon. Under the influence of this state, actions are performed that are totally at variance with the usual character of their performer. To put forward such a theory in connexion with the saints is generally regarded as a disparagement of them, just as to say that in some cases they suffered from hysteria serves only to raise a storm. Hysteria, dissociation of personality, neurosis, are terms which provoke opposition because those who object to them do not generally appreciate their significance: they are understood in a sense that goes far beyond their true meaning, and it is consequently supposed that some denigration of the person in question is intended. Far from it. In fact, to propound such a theory as an explanation of some of the odd happenings in the lives of God's servants means, on a last analysis, showing them in their true light and demonstrating that their holiness was not just something with which they were endowed from their earliest years which lasted throughout life, protecting them from the struggles, difficulties and temptations of ordinary humanity, but was the result of a hard struggle; the greater the difficulties that they overcame, then, the greater the holiness. Those who object to this explanation appear to make the saints hardly human at all, and certainly no example or encouragement to the rest of us, who are beset not only with temptations and difficulties that have been common to all ages but to the particular maladies of this present age when increasing material comfort in all walks of life seems to make us peculiarly prone to psychological difficulties of one sort and another.

To say, then, that Abbé Vianney, under the tension, the very great tension, of a daily life of incredible hardship and the acute conflict which was with him from his adolescence, together with the conflicts of others which were poured into his ears morning, noon and night, the burden of sin which he had to hear daily and all the troubles of afflicted humanity which were increasingly brought to his notice in one form or another, sometimes collapsed under the strain and showed evidence of a state that is associated in men's minds with a form of mental illness, is surely no denigration of him. Very largely, I believe, it was his own interior conflict which was at the bottom of the *Grappin* manifestations.

Under this term I refer not to that conflict that has to be endured by all practising Christians, between the "old man" in us, as St Paul puts it, and the "new", on the outcome of which depends our salvation and place in heaven, but to that struggle between a tendency and a temptation to seek to escape from circumstances which had become well nigh unbearable and his conviction as to where his duty lay. We have seen evidence of this more than once in his life. The first clear instance is the occasion of his military service when without difficulty he was persuaded to desert; it is easy to justify his conduct and to say that, after all, circumstances in those days were not what they are now, that desertion was common and almost tolerated, but the fact remains that he did desert—and his illness in the barracks at Lyon was the first step, an unconscious but extremely effective one. And he afterwards deserted with no thought of the trouble that it would bring on his father and the loss that it would cause him in the way of fines.

The pilgrimage undertaken to Louvesc, encouraged by Abbé Balley, was in its fashion a running away from his difficulties: what young man at grips with the intricacies of the Latin language and imagining them insuperable would not jump at the chance of an outing of that kind? It was turned to good use: it gave him time to see what he had to do and he came back to his books with renewed courage and determination, but it has to be remembered that there were other dullards in the class who conquered their natural repugnance without going on a pilgrimage. When he was sent away from the seminary he was justified in feeling discouraged; here again, however, he does not do the obvious thing, return to Abbé Balley and see what could be done. He runs off to the Marist Brothers and asks to join them. In this way, he imagined, he would escape the world and live in a religious atmosphere without all the burden of difficult studies. Abbé Balley encouraged him to persevere in aspiring to the priesthood, and eventually, as we have seen, he was ordained. So far, it must be admitted, he has failed to face his difficulties on at least three important occasions.

His life as a priest at Ars was one continual struggle against his "temptation" to the solitary life. He was not looking for an easier life—though in all conscience a Trappist's existence was "feather-bedded" in comparison with his—but the opportunity to weep over his "poor life" and his sins and prepare himself for death. He was haunted by this idea, obsessed by it, and sometimes the obsession obtained the upper hand. On three occasions he slipped out and tried to escape to some solitude, though towards the end of his life he saw that the only solitude that was to be his was that of the confessional. Here again we have to look deeper to determine the causes of the obsession. He was not really acquainted with the monastic life but regarded it as the ideal way of obtaining those opportunities for prayer and especially for penance that, he felt, he greatly needed.

The obsession for solitude was inextricably bound up with the idea of his own inadequacy as a priest. He was fond of insisting on the fact that few parish priests had been canonized and he looked on the office as a state of very great danger for his soul. To give it all up, to escape and spend the rest of his life weeping over his sins, appeared the solution to all his difficulties. Yet this conflict that went on in him for many years was, it appears, fundamentally the result of an inadequate response to the demands of life causing in some degree a certain maladjustment to its problems and situations. It is no denigration of Abbé Vianney to assert this. On the contrary, it shows him to have endured for many years acute trial, to have suffered in a way that many people have to suffer. To sum up the situation in another way: the *Grappin* manifestations, the result of his interior conflict, were unconsciously caused by him, though in the present state of our knowledge we cannot say how. Some would assert that at least certain of the manifestations were directly, though unconsciously, perpetrated by Abbé Vianney, others would say that they were caused by a projection of his interior conflict—the conflict seeking physical form in the rappings and the rest which occurred.

It has been said, as was mentioned above, that in these poltergeist phenomena almost invariably the presence of an adolescent is to be found. It would be nearer the truth, perhaps, to say that the constant is a person in the throes of some acute psychological conflict—a boy or girl in the adolescent stage, particularly if there is some maladjustment, is obviously in this category—and the possibility of such a conflict occurring among those whose lives are set within an especially religious context should need no pointing out.

Fr Thurston in one of his essays comes to a conclusion that seems to point in the same direction:

> One dislikes to use the word hysteria, because "hysterical" has become, beyond hope of recovery, a term of disparagement. But the more I have opportunities of studying the subject, the more convinced I become that we must recognize a class of pious—even, it may be, heroically courageous and holy— people, in whom the creations of their own thought, whether auto-suggested or hetero-suggested, dominate the entire field of consciousness, just as the figments of a dream take possession of the whole man in sleep. Such people seem easily to pass into a state of ecstasy which bears an extremely close resemblance to the trance induced by hypnosis, and, as occasionally happens in the hypnotic trance, they acquire strange powers, notably of clairvoyance and sometimes of telekinesis.[1]

On this showing, then, Abbé Vianney's trial, which was with him for many years, was one of the means by which he achieved holiness. For the saints must build up their sanctity with the materials at their disposal; in bearing this trial and eventually overcoming it, he had at hand an admirable means of mortification, but it was even more than that. Everyone, every Christian, has to achieve heaven with (or in spite of) the temperament with which he is endowed, just as his physical constitution, his mental gifts or deficiencies all have a part to play in what he makes of his life. They all have to be harnessed to the achievement of heaven. It may be a tendency to swift anger that has to be overcome (as it was with St Vincent de Paul), a genius for organization to be used to the full, or, as in Abbé Vianney's case, a psychological difficulty that must be borne; whatever it is it forms the raw materials of sanctity. Saints are human, and so they must be depicted; on the

---

[1] Reprinted in *Surprising Mystics*, ed. by J. H. Crehan, S.J. (London, 1955), p. 187.

other hand to portray them as men and women who were exempted from the common trials of humanity is a belittling of their achievement and of authentic sanctity. "Grace", we are told, "builds on nature." For that reason it is important to show the natural element of a man's life in its true perspective for it forms the material to be hewn into shape by grace. The interior obstacles of Abbé Vianney's personal temperament and the sufferings caused by it became the raw materials of his progressive sanctification.

In connexion with these trials of his own temperament it is useful to consider the profound psychological pessimism that he displayed. It is a not uncommon feature of the French character and is particularly noticeable in the years immediately preceding and following the Revolution, especially in religious circles. It was partly engendered by the prevailing Jansenistic attitude to life—if as a heresy Jansenism was dead it had nonetheless left its deep imprint on the French religious scene—though its roots go back a couple of hundred years or so before the end of the eighteenth century. It is exemplified in the deformation of the Cistercian ideal by de Rancé with his morbid insistence on penance almost as an end in itself, by Dom Le Masson's not dissimilar influence on the Carthusians; neither of these men were Jansenists but they exemplified the prevailing spirit. And it is to be found running through much of the religious writing of the French eighteenth century. Benedict Labre in his uncle's presbytery, like Jean-Marie Vianney in Abbé Balley's, found books which, in general, were of a severity and gloominess that has to be read to be believed.

The whole spirit permeating the *Rituel de Toulon* is the same. It was certainly not the book to give the man inclined to pessimism; in well-turned periods it contrived to inculcate an approach to religion that was of the gloomiest. Abbé Vianney's training for the priesthood, founded on this book and Abbé Balley's oral teaching, was hardly likely to have been a help to him in resolving his conflict.

Of the other unusual phenomena of his life little need be said. The reading of men's minds, the cures and predictions are things that can be found in other contexts besides those of sanctity.

Gradually we are coming to see that powers of this nature, start-ling as they very often are, form part of man's spiritual nature which on occasion as it were peeps through into the outside world. The striking fact about these powers in connexion with the saints is that in their case they appear much more strongly, their action is more positive than in others. Compare Abbé Vianney in the con-fessional telling a man that it is forty-four years since his last con-fession and all the mumbo-jumbo with a crystal or a pack of cards of even the most authentic of "clairvoyants". Here, what-ever the exact description of the genesis of these powers, their importance lies in their religious context; it is their religious significance that requires emphasis.

For something like thirty years, then, this country priest in the unimportant village of Ars continued to draw crowds from all over France and further afield. His time was never his own, he was besieged by penitents by day and by night, and all the time he had his own troubles to bear, the searing interior conflict that sometimes gave rise to the phenomena that we have considered, the doubts and fears about his salvation, the conviction, at times overwhelming, that he must leave it all and find solitude (not peace) where he could bewail his "poor life" and prepare for death.

All that he harnessed eventually to the service of God, going on to almost his dying day with the confessions and the torturing daily round. He had little time for prayer, as ordinary people know it, but his whole existence was turned Godwards so that prayer became for him a state. To read the books written about the religious life and prayer, with their emphasis on the pursuit of perfection, on the stages of prayer, on acquiring virtue and so on, is, when we think of a life like Abbé Vianney's, to be plunged into a world of unreality. His was no text-book life, save in its final achievement, for his method was utterly different from the com-plications of some writers on mysticism: his was the simplicity of the Gospel—he loved God with his whole being, and his life reflected it. And because of this love he was enabled, finally, to resolve his conflicts and to carry on to the end of his life that work that he was doing for God. His entire existence as a parish priest displayed heroism of an unusual quality.

Heroic sanctity is the qualification for canonization. In the biographies of the saints it is not unusual to provide a chapter on the heroicity of the subject's virtues—his faith, hope and charity and so on—but here it seems unnecessary to enter into so technical a discussion. Abbé Vianney's devotion to his duty as a priest is plain for all to see, his humility stands out throughout his life. He has appeared, in these pages, as a stern and unrelenting pastor on occasion, frequently as a confessor of severity, though in his later years he became far milder in dealing with penitents, a man hard with himself and expecting a high standard with others. But it would be a mistake to try to fit him into a mould, to transform him into the conventional (and not very attractive), rather self-conscious, certainly efficient but somewhat inhuman and humourless ecclesiastical type that seems to emerge from the manuals of instruction intended for seminarists and young priests. In the first place he thought nothing of his own dignity (remember the canon's cape), and then he could laugh at himself, and he did so frequently. He sometimes teased his curates and penitents, and if his brand of humour strikes one as elementary it must be remembered that he remained at heart an unsophisticated peasant.

Abbé Vianney was that uncomfortable type, the man with a mission. Primarily it consisted in the revival of religion in his parish and then wherever his influence could reach. So it is not extraordinary that his whole life seems dominated by his sense of the enormity of sin. He compared the priest (and he had himself in mind) to St Peter in Pilate's judgement hall, a constant spectator while our Lord is insulted, mocked and ill-treated. Rarely he tasted the delights of the mystical life and for long periods he was without consolation, praying and working in a state of utter desolation, so that it was not for nothing that writing to his bishop he signed *J. M. B. Vianney, pauvre malheureux prêtre.*

All this was the price that he paid for carrying out his mission —how far he took upon himself the penance and mortification that should have been performed by his penitents heaven alone knows—to the very end, all his energies devoted to the one purpose of serving others and through them God, humbly, perseveringly, with no thought of self, taking back nothing that he had given, striving always to convince men of the enormity of sin and to draw them to the love of their Creator. All this he did, enduring his heavy trial, at grips with an interior conflict that permeated his whole life. He had his burden to bear and he bore it, using it as a means to holiness, by its agency advancing along his path heaven-wards, and when he was without it at last, he had nearly achieved his goal.

CHAPTER XIV

THE LAST YEARS

IN the pulpit at Ars on one occasion towards the end of his life Abbé Vianney, preaching on the submissive acceptance of trials and tribulations, mentioned a case known to him. "I know some-one", he said, "who knows how to accept crosses, heavy crosses, and who carries them lovingly. . . . it is Mlle Jaricot." Her name must have been familiar to many in the congregation, and we have seen how, in his early years as a priest, Abbé Vianney made con-tact with her and how he owed to her his devotion to St Philomena and the relic of the saint. To the end of his life Pauline Jaricot remained in touch with him. The great work that she founded at Lyon in 1809, known as the Association for the Propagation of the Faith, had been established on a firm footing and was prospering. Not so Pauline Jaricot. To bodily sufferings were added others. Through the fraud of another she had lost her fortune in an enter-prise founded to help the working classes and, what was worse in her opinion, by inviting the collaboration of other, small inves-tors, had involved them in loss also, and was unable to repay them. "I fear debt more greatly than death", she wrote once, but debt was to be her portion to the end of her days. Her friends would not help her and she had to suffer slander and derision; she was desti-tute, and in 1855 was obliged to register as a pauper. Through all her trials, borne meekly and uncomplainingly, Abbé Vianney encouraged her and did what he could to help her.

In the cold February of 1859 she arrived in Ars with a com-panion; both women were cold, wet through and hungry. The east wind was blowing and snow was on the ground. Abbé Vianney welcomed them in his room where with some damp logs he endeavoured to make a fire, but no sooner was it lit than it went out again. "Don't worry about the cold," Pauline besought him, "but please warm my poor soul with a few sparks of faith and hope."

What had Abbé Vianney to offer her in the way of consolation? He himself had known many long periods of desolation and in addition was continually weighed down with the burden of the sins of others which served only to increase his acute perception of the evil of sin. Small wonder that predominantly he was sad. Yet with Pauline he knew that he was dealing with a soul who needed something more than the precepts that he was usually obliged to preach. For the last few years of his life, in fact, his catechism lessons and his sermons had all been reduced to their simplest point. He spoke of the love of God; it was a topic that he seemed unable to avoid. Whatever his subject it was not long before some phrase, some consideration distracted him from it and recalled to him what had become the central theme of all his teaching. And so he talked to Pauline Jaricot, a smile playing round his lips, his tired eyes lighting up as he warmed to his theme. Though his words were ordinary, though the ideas were by no means novel, yet there was nothing banal about what he had to say because he spoke of what he knew by experience. Pauline Jaricot left Ars comforted, but material destitution remained her lot for the rest of her days until her death in 1862. By this time her friend and comforter at Ars was already in the grave.

Abbé Vianney during his lifetime must have handled large sums of money. Alms poured in from the pilgrims, and in his latter years as parish priest of Ars he did not need to resort to the devices —anticipating payment of his patrimony, for example—that were necessary in his earlier years. Yet neither then nor later was any of the money for himself or his personal needs. It all went to help the poor, to embellish his church, to establish foundations which should ensure that missions were regularly preached in the surrounding countryside. The conversion of Ars had been his first concern. Once that had been achieved, with the result that pilgrims began to come to see the priest who had effected it, he sought to convert the whole district in addition to all who travelled from great distances to obtain his help or advice. The means that he employed for the local parishes was the establishment of regular missions.

Pre-eminently, indeed, he was a man with a mission, and like all such, he had his moments of discouragement—with some of the results that we have seen—and experienced a sense of urgency that made him shorten his nights to less than the barest minimum of sleep that was necessary for health; every minute counted. Yet what stands out in his lifework is especially the absence of fuss. There were, of course, none of the "stunts", the attempts at personal publicity that we seem nowadays to take for granted among those in the public eye; nor were there any of the attributes of the popular "hot-gospeller". Quietly and with dignity he set about his work, which was on a scale that probably no parish priest has ever been obliged to undertake. In the last year of his life Ars was invaded by upwards of one hundred thousand pilgrims; the mere physical labour involved in hearing their confessions and preaching to them would be enough to last most men several years.

After his last attempted flight from the parish he seems to have come finally into calm waters, and his last five or six years were free from the distressing manifestations of conflict that we see in his earlier life. He achieved serenity, that serenity which is the final mark of the unitive life at its highest degree, and it is of this period that reports are current of his being seen in ecstasy, and of bright light shining from his confessional. But the secret of his growth in sanctity and of his whole inner life is guarded by the best of bastions, the genuine deep humility which is itself also one of the signs of the presence of holiness.

He did what he was told over the matter of eating; perhaps, since his last illness, he realized that he could not go on with his work if he did not husband his strength. For he still had much to do, and truth to tell he was in no shape to do it. He was so thin that he gave the impression of being a ghost, his hands and his face so shrunken that he seemed discarnate. His cough had not left him since his last illness and as the years went on it became worse; it appeared to shake his whole frame, and three or four times an hour during his short night it so racked him that he was obliged to get up. He crept about now, holding on to what he could.

All about him did their best to help. Abbé Toccanier and the brothers, the nuns that had taken over his *Providence*, Catherine

Lassagne and devout women who had come to settle in Ars plied him with their attentions; he was grateful, but so far as he could went on as in the past. In 1855 he revealed that he sometimes felt giddy. Abbé Toccanier had written off to the bishop asking that Abbé Vianney might be dispensed from the breviary on account of his immense labours and his great infirmities. The bishop replied that he forbade him to say the breviary whenever it was not allowed by the curate, and that he, the bishop, would say it in his name and that the Curé d'Ars could offer his sufferings for the bishop's intention. Abbé Vianney managed to say his office on most days, but could no longer do so kneeling down as had been his habit. Someone told him of the excellence of the Roman breviary and he expressed a wish to use that instead of the local one that he had said since his ordination. Abbé Toccanier decided to give him a copy and wrote off to Paris post haste for one to be sent; his intention was that after the Curé's death it should revert to him and thus he would be in possession of an interesting and valuable relic. But a colleague pointed out that the Roman breviary with its eighteen psalms at Sunday Matins and the long one hundred and eighteenth psalm for the little hours daily was much longer than that of Belley; since Abbé Vianney found difficulty in saying the latter he would do well not to change it for one of greater length.

The church at Ars, which had been his constant concern to embellish since his arrival in the village, seemed to him now to be far too small for the needs of the villagers and pilgrims; and he wanted to honour St Philomena with a fine building that should express his gratitude to her and his confidence in her intercession. He spent some time talking it over with an architect—Pierre Bossan—who produced a plan; Abbé Vianney paid the fee by presenting him with a rosary of coral beads on a golden chain. Of course there was no money in hand for the undertaking. A subscription list was opened, headed by Abbé Vianney's subscription of one thousand francs (forty pounds). "I will pray to God," he managed to scratch out on paper, "for all those who help me to build a fine church to St Philomena." These were the last lines he wrote. They are dated 2 April 1859.

He never saw the church; it was left to his successor as Curé d'Ars (Abbé Toccanier) to start the project, which was brought to completion under the second successor, Mgr Convert. This is the church that is nowadays to be seen by the pilgrims to Ars. At the apse of the old church there was added a transept and a monstrosity of a basilica, a great mass of stone and ornament towering over the little church that was Abbé Vianney's, expressive of the taste of a generation that could be responsible for the Sacré Coeur at Montmartre or the basilica at Fourvière. All that can be said of it is that Abbé Vianney would probably have liked it. After his death, to obtain the funds required appeals were sent out far and wide and a lottery was organized the two chief prizes of which were the late Curé's prieu-dieu and his watch. This enterprise brought in four thousand pounds.

In 1859 this venture was in the future and Abbé Vianney was still dragging himself about and talking of death to come at an early date. In the pulpit he was almost inaudible, yet the crowds still flocked to his instructions, possibly in greater numbers because it was felt that he would not last much longer, and still came away from the sight of him consoled and comforted; still he wrought conversions, though his words in the confessional became increasingly difficult to distinguish as his failing strength and almost complete absence of teeth rendered his speech little more than a confused mumble. His hearing was acute to the end; that sense at least, the most important to a confessor, remained with him. When at eleven he came out from the penitents and went to the tribune for the instruction that he had given daily for many years it was seen how frail and weak he was. He could hardly articulate his words and his ideas seemed to be expressed in a series of exclamations; frequently he was racked by coughing fits and often he was in tears. Yet it was to hear this man, to confess to him, that crowds travelled many, in some cases thousands, of miles.

Catherine Lassagne watched over him and did what she could to alleviate his cough and general weakness. He was obviously a difficult patient. She saw to it that he had his hot milk in the evening and once wrung from him an acknowledgement that her insistence on his drinking it at an earlier hour had enabled him to get through the day without collapsing.

His nights were disturbed by his cough and frequently he was bathed in sweat. Every morning he found it increasingly hard to leave his bed and returned to his work in the confessional with the greatest difficulty. He was seventy-three and looked at least twenty years older, yet never on one occasion did he prolong his night's rest. "I wanted to sleep on this morning," he confessed once, "but I had no hesitation in getting up. The salvation of souls is of the utmost importance." At another time, when told by Abbé Toccanier that he looked tired, he remarked: "Oh, the sinners will kill the sinner in the end!" He had to fight against sleep in the confessional. Sometimes he was momentarily overcome and penitents would have mercy on him for a few minutes and wait while he rested. Yet in spite of all this and being harassed continually by the crowds it was usually with a smile on his face that he presented himself to the world, a picture of serenity. Tears came occasionally, in the pulpit, and in private, as when he told Abbé Toccanier that even if it were necessary for him to remain on earth until the end of the world he would still get up at midnight. "I'm not frightened by fatigue," he concluded. "I should be the happiest of priests if it were not for the thought that I must come before God's judgement seat as a parish priest." And the tears began to fall. Yet the fear at dying a parish priest no longer troubled him to the extent of giving him doubts about his vocation.

Ever since his attempted flight in 1853 he had spoken of his approaching end; in 1858 he mentioned it as occurring the next year. In 1859 in July he spoke of it as very near. To Mme Pauze of Saint-Etienne, who had informed him of her pilgrimage to Louvesc, he remarked, in answer to the fear expressed by her that she would not see him again, "Indeed, my child, we shall meet again in three weeks!"

It has been said that, in the nave of the little church at Ars, during the winter the waiting penitents were frozen and during the summer they were baked. In the confessional these extremes of temperature were still more acute. All through the extreme heat of

July 1859 Abbé Vianney persevered, only leaving the confessional at his accustomed times, whereas at intervals the penitents could go out of the church to obtain a breath of air.

July 29 was a Friday. On getting up he felt worse than usual but was in the confessional by one in the morning; the heat of the church, combined with the burning fever of his body, compelled him to leave several times in order to rest for a few moments in front of the presbytery. At eleven in the morning he asked for a few drops of wine to help him get through his catechism lesson, but he was completely inaudible, only his gestures betraying that he was speaking of his habitual topic, our Lord in the eucharist and his love for mankind. That evening on his way back to the presbytery he was bent nearly double, and fainted at the foot of the stairs. Eventually he reached his room and was assisted to bed by Br Jerome. Shortly after midnight he knocked. Catherine Lassagne, who had remained on watch in the next room in spite of strict injunctions that he was to be left alone in the presbytery, went in. "It is my poor end," Abbé Vianney managed to whisper. "You must get the Curé of Jassans." Br Jerome came to keep watch and spoke of finding a doctor as well as a priest. "No, it is useless," was the reply. "It is my poor end; the doctor can do nothing." Abbé Toccanier, who had been sent for, suggested that St Philomena would obtain a cure. "Oh, St Philomena will be able to do nothing!"

At daybreak Abbé Beau of Jassans and Dr Saunier arrived. The latter was pessimistic. "If it gets a little cooler there is some small hope, but if this heat continues we shall lose him," he remarked. With the usual unfeeling selfishness of crowds the pilgrims besieged the presbytery. Some managed even to pentrate to the sick man's bedroom and there make their confessions. Abbé Vianney seems to have had no doubt that he would not recover and during his last confession told Abbé Beau that he was ready to die. He had no complaints; he did as he was told, taking medicine and meekly accepting the treatment prescribed by the doctor in a way quite unlike his usual attitude.

Some privileged penitents, his own parishioners, the brothers and the nuns managed still to penetrate to the sick-room. Most of the pilgrims remained crowded together before the presbytery door or in the church. They were told that Abbé Vianney sent his blessing, and from time to time a bell was rung to indicate that at that moment he was raising his hand in benediction. In order to offset the great heat which still continued some of the parishioners stretched sheets over the roof of the presbytery and kept them watered. Abbé Vianney lay still on his bed; his lips hardly moved, only occasionally did he make a short remark. "I have only thirty-six francs left," he murmured on the morning of 2 August. "See that they are given to the doctor and tell him not to come again. I shan't be able to pay him." Later in the day he encouraged Abbé Toccanier about the building of the new church. "You'll be worried about it for three years," he told him. Three years to the day almost Abbé Toccanier found that he had enough money in hand to begin on the building.

The heat continued and the patient grew weaker. In the afternoon it was decided to give him the last sacraments. As the procession entered the room he struggled into a sitting position, and with tears in his eyes, received viaticum and the last anointing. The room was so hot that the attendant clergy were obliged to put out their candles. He was ready now to die, he felt, and it might be thought that he would have been allowed to pass his last few hours in peace and undisturbed. But the parishioners of Ars were worried that when they lost their Curé they would lose also his body, for in 1855 he had made a will leaving it to the disposal of the Bishop of Belley; the people of Ars could not be sure that it would be left in their keeping. The lawyer from Trévoux was sent for and, on Wednesday, 3 August, at a moment when it was perceived that Abbé Vianney had momentarily rallied, a party of five—the lawyer and four witnesses—was ushered into the sick-room. "Where do you wish to be buried?" demanded the lawyer. "At Ars," Abbé Vianney managed to gasp out, "but my body is not of any importance . . ."

On the evening of the same day came the bishop. Abbé Vianney recognized him but was unable to do more than indicate his thanks for the visit. He could not utter a word.

At two the next morning (Thursday, 4 August), as the prayers for the dying were being recited by his bedside, Abbé Vianney "rendered his soul to God without a struggle". At this moment the storm which had been brewing for the last day or two broke, so that he breathed his last to the sound of thunder and the flash of lightning. He was seventy-three and had been parish priest of Ars for a little over forty-one years. The sorrow of the people of Ars, who went about muttering "Our holy Curé is dead", was soon shared by the whole world. Immediately the roads leading to Ars were black with the crowds of pilgrims from the surrounding countryside and further afield; for forty-eight hours there was an uninterrupted procession past his body laid out in cassock, rochet and stole in the downstairs room in the presbytery.

During his lifetime no one had been able to induce him to pose for his photograph. A picture was taken, however, when he was laid out. The funeral was held on Saturday, 6 August, in the presence of an immense crowd, and the panegyric was preached by the bishop. The body was finally buried in the nave with the inscription CI-GIT JEAN-MARIE-BAPTISTE VIANNEY, CURÉ D'ARS. The pilgrimage which did not come to an end after his death, the miracles, the beatification and canonization are important events in the history of the Church but can form no part of the life story of the person chiefly concerned. A biography should end with its subject's death.

*   *   *

The immense changes everywhere in the world during the century that has elapsed since Abbé Vianney's death, however, compel us to consider his relevance to these times, for in reading his life, in dwelling on his achievements, we are apt to be struck by the fact that he appears to us to belong to a wholly different epoch. Can he mean anything to this age of supersonic flight and nuclear energy? After all, he lived when men were reaping the fruits of the eighteenth century, "the age of reason", in times of rapid change not so very unlike our own in some respects, when the faith of many was pinned ever hopefully on the material; he offered them the challenge of the spiritual, of utter faith in God and the example of a life wholly founded on this faith. From his niche in the calendar of the Church he continues to offer the same challenge to us of the second half of the twentieth century. In his own day he was outstanding as a priest, and for this reason has been made patron of parish priests, but he was outstanding even more as a Christian, a witness to Christ in a world seemingly set on the way to faithlessness. Modern man seems to have been in-oculated against Christianity by minute doses of it and needs the massive injection of the saints' example to enable him to overcome his tolerance. Abbé Vianney's example was effective in this way in his own day—it was principally what he was rather than what he did that drew men to him—and still the lesson of his life can show men the meaning of real Christianity.

To priests he offers the example of a priestly life of complete devotion to his calling and to his flock, even after it had grown to the size that we have seen in this book, even when he was on his deathbed. He was ungifted, humanly speaking, a peasant without influence or learning, dumped in the least important parish of the diocese, where he remained without preferment for upwards of forty years, transforming it into the most frequented and best-known parish in the country by the mute-eloquence of his holiness. Such an example needs no explaining, such a life needs no pointing of the moral. "God grant," wrote St Pius X, "that every priest may follow [Abbé Vianney's] example. . . . May all parish priests remember [his] example and imitate the ardent charity which urges us to despise all things, even life itself." So it is that thinking of his example of charity and humility we can forget the basilica that offends the eye, the place where his poor "body" lies ("my body is not of any importance," he said), with its too intricately worked and over-elaborated metal shrine surmounted by an un-convincing St Philomena and supported by figures of SS. John the Baptist, Benedict Labre, Francis of Assisi and Francis Regis. Nor need you visit the "Chapel of the Heart" where at a little distance from the presbytery the parish priests of the world by their donations have caused to be erected the kind of shrine to contain his heart that is to be expected in the circumstances.

At least the presbytery has preserved something of the essential

Abbé Vianney, the peasant-style house, the rough walls, the poor possessions, the few books, the large breviary. The shrine in the church contains the body, though it is vested in a cassock of silk, a rochet of lace such as he never would have worn (remember the canon's cape), and his hands are clasping a bejewelled rosary such as he would have given away on the spot. But the face is preserved by its mask of wax, and you can look on those features as they were at the end of his life—the long straight line of the mouth, the face of a man tried and proved by suffering, the eyes just perceptible through the thin lids, the long, finely wrought nose, but the face of a man who found peace through following his vocation though sorely tempted to abandon it for the peace of monastic life. You see the deep furrows on either cheek that seem channels eroded by the tears over men's sins, and his own supposed inadequacy for his task, and you can consider the final achievement of this man who was at first regarded as a misfit by some of his colleagues in the clergy. The man appears almost to glow through the wax covering of the features. It seems to be the light of holiness shining through the dead shell. Would he have been pleased with what has been done with his body, the honour bestowed on it, the finery with which it is clad? Hardly, one supposes. Yet he would have smiled, I think, at the thought that men were honouring parish priests in his person—as he often remarked, there are so few of them officially in heaven.

INDEX